Rural Alaska Teacher's Moving Guide

Rural Alaska Teacher's Moving Guide

What to Expect on the Last Frontier

Wally Rose

Third Stream Press

Valdez   •   Ponte Vedra

ISBN-13: 978-1500275044
ISBN-10: 1500275042

Third Stream Press
P.O. Box 2975
Valdez, Alaska 99686

www.thirdstreampress.com

Rural Alaska Teacher's Moving Guide

Contents

Foreword

A few days ago, Mrs. Rose (my wife of 20+ years) received a text from a friend in the lower 48. The text concluded with the letters "IMHO." As any Gen-Xer or Millennial knows, those letters stand for "In My Humble Opinion." As a baby-boomer myself, this strikes me as a particularly polite way to end a conversation. The writer is saying, "This is how I see the situation. You may not agree with me, but you decided to read this far. I don't claim to know everything, but you asked, and here's what I think."

So, let me preface this book with a great big IMHO. In fact, you could probably place those letters at the beginning of many of the paragraphs in this book. IMHO, you need a nice waterproof rain jacket. IMHO, you need some waterproof boots. IMHO, you should leave your big flat-screen TV in the lower 48. This book is basically one IMHO after another.

But, it's an informed humble opinion. I live in rural Alaska. I teach in a village school. I've made a few mistakes along the way, and I've learned a lot about living far away from my familiar territory (the southeastern United States.) When it comes to moving to rural Alaska, my IMHO is based on experience. I'm not claiming that my experiences are universal to Alaska bush teaching. But they are typical. If your research and experience leads to different conclusions, I encourage you to publish as well, and add to the core knowledge base.

Let me tell you a little more about myself. I am a male with more than 25 years of teaching experience. I am older than 45, but not yet 60. I am not especially athletic, but I am in decent physical health, and I enjoy outdoor activities. I graduated from a major university with a degree in education, and got the master's degree going to school at night, before online classes were invented. College classes left me with three areas of certification on my teaching license, and I studied, took state exams, and added three more certification areas over the last 10 years. I have taught required classes and electives at most grade levels, and I have enjoyed almost all of my teaching experiences. My wife and I decided to move to rural Alaska, seeking new adventures and experiences. We had vacationed in Alaska twice before, and we researched the different parts of the state online for about three years before making the move.

My wife, Mrs. Rose, has been my faithful companion and confidant for more than half my life. She was a full-time Mom for our only child, and is in charge of running the household. I hope you can tell that I write this with the greatest respect for stay-at-home moms. Any teacher with any experience can tell you the value of such a dedicated presence in the home.

In the interest of transparency, I will tell you that Wally Rose is a pen name, not my real name. I decided to use a pseudonym to protect my privacy, and to deflect any conflict if you disagree with my advice in this book. I hope that you respect that decision.

My desire as a teacher and a writer is to provide you with some useful information. To keep costs down, this book is self-published, with just enough profit margin to provide financial motivation to work on a computer when I could be outside in beautiful Alaska. I am certain that you will recoup the purchase price of this book many times over with the advice that I provide you.

Certainly, you understand that my desire in writing this book is to help you make a smooth transition from life in the lower 48 to your new home in rural Alaska. I remember when I attended my district's new teacher orientation, finding myself in a room filled with "newly-minted" teachers younger than my daughter. If you fit in that group – recent college graduates – you can think of me as your Uncle Wally. This book has the advice that your parents would give you if they had experience moving to Alaska.

When you arrive at your school location, you will likely find willing mentors to help you adjust to village life. Until you meet those mentors, my hope is that this book will help you prepare for the experience of a lifetime.

In my humble opinion.

Introduction

So, You Want to Move to Rural Alaska?

Just exactly what does that mean? Rural Alaska living can mean many things, but to most people, rural Alaska means "not on the road system."

If you take a look at a highway map of the state of Alaska, you'll see that there are roads connecting the cities and towns in the eastern part of the state. Alaska map distances can be deceiving, because Alaska is such a large state. But, a person could start driving in Homer (the locals call it "the end of the road") on the Kenai Peninsula, head north to Soldotna, then east through Sterling and Cooper Landing, and north to Portage, and eventually Anchorage, the state's largest city. From Anchorage, you could drive north to Denali and Fairbanks, then east on the Alaska Highway to Delta Junction, Tok, and eventually Canada. An eastern route out of Anchorage leads to Glenallen, Copper Center, and Valdez. Sure, there's a lot of wilderness in between these cities and towns, but they are all on "the road system." People who live there can drive from one community to another to purchase supplies, visit family members, or just get out of town for a few days.

Now, look at the western part of Alaska. There are no highways in the entire western half of the state. There are a few medium-sized towns in the area. Bethel, with about 6,000 residents is the state's 9th largest city. But you can't drive to Bethel. All people and goods must arrive by air, or by barge.

The same concept holds true for southeastern Alaska. Residents in Juneau can drive to a few destinations, and the Alaska Marine Highway ferry system services many of the southeastern communities. But there are many areas of southeastern Alaska that you just can't reach in a car.

Rural Alaska is the area not serviced by the road system. This part of Alaska is commonly called "the bush." Even short trips, such as the 13 mile jaunt from Bethel to the village of Kwethluk, are made by small plane (or snow machine for brave souls in the winter.)

This book focuses on moving to villages in the Alaska bush – communities not on the road system, and accessible only by small plane, boat, or snow machine.

Some bush communities, such as Bethel, Dillingham, and Nome, fit that definition, but function as regional hubs. They enjoy larger schools, grocery stores, and restaurants. Although moving to a remote hub presents its share of challenges, they aren't quite as drastic as moving to a small village. By my definition, if you can walk into a bank, buy a variety of fresh produce, or get Chinese take-out, you technically aren't in the bush, no matter how you got there.

This book is about preparing for village life. No Burger King. No beauty salon. No Baskin-Robbins. Domino's doesn't deliver out here!

The Decision is Yours

One thing I'm not going to do in this book is encourage you to move to rural Alaska, or discourage you from making the move. The decision is yours, and can really only be made by you and your immediate family. If you talk to enough people, and read enough online postings, you will find teachers who moved to Alaska 20 years ago, love it, raised their children in the bush, and couldn't imagine living anywhere else. You will also find teachers who left the bush screaming after a couple of months, and returned to the lower 48. Whether you decide to stay in Alaska for several years, for a year or two, or decide not to go at all – that's your decision to make. I wouldn't try to make that decision for you, and no one else should want to, either.

My guess is that if you're reading this book, you are at least leaning toward seeking an Alaska teaching job. My hope is that you will be better prepared for the journey after reading this book. The move itself, and all of the changes it will bring will be challenging enough. Understanding the importance of waterproof shoes should make the transition a little bit easier.

Alaska Teaching = Alaska + Teaching

This makes sense, I know. But have you really thought about it? Let's take a minute.

You will be in Alaska.

There are no two ways about it. You will wake-up in Alaska every day, and go to sleep in Alaska at night. You will work in Alaska, play in Alaska, and shop in Alaska. The people you have face-to-face conversations with will be in Alaska. The people you hug, high-five, and pat on the back will be in Alaska. The shoulders you cry on will be Alaska shoulders. If you don't want to be in Alaska, then you shouldn't be an Alaska teacher.

You will be a teacher.

You will work in a school, with children, at least five days a week. You will probably work a few evenings and weekends, too. You will plan lessons, teach, and grade papers. You may also tie shoes, hold tissues for nose-blowing, and open milk cartons. You will have parent conferences, host afternoon detention, and chaperone the school dance. This is what teachers do. If you don't want to be a teacher, then you shouldn't be an Alaska teacher.

Yes, you will probably be able to visit relatives over Christmas break, and most teachers leave for the summer. You can order things online, and Skype, e-mail and text your friends. You can update your Facebook page daily. You will have time to ride an ATV, hike tundra trails, fish for salmon, and maybe even see the Northern Lights. But first and foremost, you will be an Alaska teacher.

Don't move to Alaska just to hunt and fish, or just to pay-off your student loans, or get as far away from your previous life as possible. There are other places to do these things, and other ways to support your adventures. You've got to want to be in Alaska, and you've got to want to teach.

That's Uncle Wally's real talk. As I wrote earlier, you need to make the best decision.

Rural Alaska is Very Different from Tourist Alaska

Alaska is a great place to take a vacation. Some people like to cruise past calving glaciers in southeast Alaska, and wear raincoats and rubber boots while walking on the Ketchikan boardwalks. Other tourists enjoy the majestic Denali National Park, with its day-long hikes and plush lodges. My personal favorite is the Kenai Peninsula. I love the sky-tram ride up Mount Alyeska, the SeaLife Center in Seward, and the funky Homer Spit.

Bush Alaska is nothing like that. Bush Alaska is beautiful and wild and free. But it is also very rugged. It is not a vacation experience. Once again, I am not discouraging you. Just make sure you realize which Alaska you're moving to. It's not the Alaska with Starbucks coffee shops and mints on the hotel pillow.

Rural Alaska is Remote

When the district personnel director interviewed me, he made sure I knew that my village did not have many of the luxuries of the city. "You know, we don't have any movie theatres out here." My wife and I rarely go to the movies. "We don't have any shopping malls out here." We try to avoid shopping malls as well. "We don't have restaurants out here." Fortunately, Mrs. Rose is a great cook, and we'll eat out when we leave the village.

But to be honest, I did not understand how remote a bush village truly is. We are a long way out here. A long way. Leaving the village requires an expensive flight on a bush plane. And unlike the depiction in the reality TV shows, the bush planes don't fly when the weather is bad. People have been stuck for days, awaiting the return flight to the village. Vacations have been delayed or canceled because no flights were leaving the village.

When you arrive in your village, you probably need to come to terms with the fact that you might not leave again until Christmas. Yes, there are opportunities to travel. One district has three weekend in-service meetings for new teachers in the fall months. If you sign-up to sponsor the cross-country or volleyball team, you might have the opportunity to fly to another village or a regional hub. But most villages aren't connected to other villages by roads or trails. (Sometimes snow machine trails are cut in the winter months, but that trip isn't recommended for beginners.) Your village could be as small as the neighborhood you grew up in. It's a lifestyle that revolves around home and community. It's about where you are, not where you want to go.

Don't Assume Any Amenities

The amenities of your hometown may exist in your bush Alaska village, but they may not. Chapter 11: Questions to Ask an Interviewer is designed to make sure you don't have any surprises when you get there. But here are a few things you might not have pondered.

Your village might not have street names, and you probably won't have a house number. You will go to the post office to get your mail, including parcels. There is no UPS or FedEx service. Some online vendors will ship to Alaska, but others won't. Some vendors will attach exorbitant shipping fees.

There will probably not be a medical doctor in your village. The dentist comes twice a year. There will not be a veterinarian.

Your principal will also be your landlord, and the school custodians will take care of the housing repairs. You might have a roommate.

Your village might not have flush toilets.

Those are a few of the things you will need to ask about. They may or may not be "deal-breakers" for you. But you need to understand as you enter the job market that certain assumptions about life in the lower 48 just can't be made here. Once again, I am not trying to discourage anyone. I just want you to go into the situation with your eyes wide open.

Topics Not Covered in this Book

Before we move on to the actual chapters, please understand that there are a few topics that I purposefully don't cover in this book.

Employment

Your best source for learning about Alaska teacher employment is the Alaska Teacher Placement web-site: http://alaskateacher.org/ This book is not intended as a "how to get a job in Alaska" manual.

Specific School Districts

I am not going to write about specific Alaska school districts. Almost all districts have comprehensive web-sites, and most of them are easy to find. The forum section of the Alaska Teacher Placement web-site provides the opportunity for job-seekers to ask such questions.

Certification

Your best source for information about Alaska teacher certification is the Alaska Department of Education web-site: http://education.alaska.gov/TeacherCertification/

They do a great job, and anything I write would pale in comparison to their expertise.

Cultural Aspects of Village Life

When you move to a bush Alaska village, you will likely live among Alaskan tribal members. Your adjustment to this culture is an important element of your job satisfaction. The principal and teachers at your school location are in the best position to help you learn about the native culture. I have found it overly simplistic to say "All Yup'ik people are this way..." or "All Athabascan people are this way..." The best way to learn about the native culture in your village is to meet the local people, keep an open mind, listen, and observe.

So, there you have it. You need to consider all of these things and more before accepting a teaching job in Alaska.

The rest of the Rural Alaska Teacher's Moving Guide is designed for those hardy souls who have decided to teach and live in the Alaska bush. My goal is to help you make a successful move to your new home village.

Chapter 1

Where Will You Live?

Housing for bush teachers

As you learn about the Alaska school districts that interest you, teacher housing should be one of your main areas of research. As an Alaska bush teacher, your choice of housing will be very limited, if any choice exists at all.

Basically, there are two possible scenarios: living in district-owned housing, and renting in the village. Chances are, your teacher contract will require one or the other. The large majority of Alaska bush teachers live in housing units owned by the school district. Most school sites have several teacher housing units near the school.

District-Owned Teacher Housing

There are many good things about living in district-owned teacher housing. The main advantage is that when moving to the Alaska bush, you won't have to worry about where you'll live. That decision will be made for you by the district. Most villages aren't set up to accommodate renters. There are no real estate offices, apartment complexes, or rental agencies.

Teacher Housing Assignments

Your principal will assign a housing unit to you, based upon availability, need and seniority. Maybe you're concerned that you'll arrive at your teaching site, and there won't be a housing unit for you. Don't be. The district's hiring decision will be based in part on how you fit into the housing scheme. For example, if you are a single person, you may be assigned to a small modular home, a duplex unit, or an apartment. If you are bringing family members, your housing assignment will be based on the size of your family.

If you are worried that you might arrive in your village with your spouse and two children, and assigned a one-bedroom apartment, don't be. That probably won't happen, because your housing needs will be discussed before the contract is offered. That system might seem to favor single teachers over teachers with families. But from my experience, most school sites have enough teacher housing for single teachers, as well as teachers with families.

You may be assigned a roommate, based on the housing available in your village. Once again, this is typically at the discretion of your school principal. Usually, single teachers far from home appreciate living with a roommate. Having a roommate will also lower your rent. Roommates can split household bills, such as Internet, landline phone, and satellite TV, should you choose to buy those services. Roommates can also share cooking and housekeeping chores. If you are a single person, and you absolutely can't stand the idea of sharing a house or apartment with a roommate, then you should let the principal know early in the hiring process. It might be that the principal has one job opening, and one bedroom in a two-bedroom housing unit available.

Condition of Teacher Housing

The condition of teacher housing units can vary greatly between districts, within the district, and even among housing units at the school site. Some housing units will be new and modern. Others will be old, and lack many of the features that you're used to at home. The main impediment for districts to upgrade teacher housing is money. Construction costs in villages are astronomical. Construction materials must be flown-in or barged, and both options are very expensive. Some villages don't have workers qualified to build houses, so construction workers must be dispatched to the village and fed and housed for the duration of the construction project. A common approach is for districts to purchase pre-fabricated housing units that are transported and assembled in the village. Once again, this is a tremendously costly endeavor. So, if your school district's teacher housing is not as fancy as your housing back home, don't be offended. The district has probably decided to forestall new construction as long as possible in order to put resources into other programs.

As a teacher candidate, you have every right to ask about the teacher housing before you accept a job. Don't get in the mindset of saying, "I need a job. I'll live anywhere!" Just as the principal will ask you many questions during the interview, you should be prepared to ask about the teacher housing at the school site.

As you investigate school districts on the Internet, look for teacher housing agreements (leases,) which are often part of the teacher contract. Most leases are quite specific about the rental rate, as it relates to the condition of the teacher housing and the features of the housing. So, if your housing is new and featured-filled, expect to pay more than your colleague who lives in an older housing unit with more primitive furnishings.

Before we leave this section, be aware that many districts have purposefully built new teacher housing to attract teaching candidates. Living in a new or nearly-new housing unit, very similar to what you would expect to rent in the lower 48, is certainly possible in the Alaska bush. But you would need to actively seek such districts and villages. Conversely, some districts prefer to offer teachers higher salaries and lower rents. They contend that there's a limited amount of money, and they put their district's money into teacher salaries instead of new housing.

As you make your final employment decision, consider teacher housing – and how much you will pay for it – as part of the total compensation package. Take a look at these three fictional scenarios:

School 1
    Salary: $48,000
    Housing: New
    Rent: $700/month

School 2
    Salary: $51,000
    Housing: Average
    Rent: $600/month

School 3
  Salary: $53,000
  Housing: Poor
  Rent: $500/month

A teacher at School 1 would get to live in a new housing unit. However, they would make $3,000 per year less than the teacher at School 2, and pay $1,000 more per year in rent. So, the real "cost" of living in the new teacher housing is $4,000 per year. The teacher who lives in poor housing while earning a higher salary would actually make $7,000 more per year ($5,000 in salary and $2,000 in lower rent) than the teacher in School 1. Once again, the choice is yours to make. As you narrow-down your choices, make sure to consider housing quality, salary, and rental payment.

Plumbing in Teacher Housing

As I wrote in this book's introduction, when you move to the Alaska bush, you need to think about things that you might not think about in your hometown in the lower 48. When it comes to your teacher housing unit, you need to ask about the plumbing and running water features.

If you went hunting for an apartment in a town or city near your college, you would expect all of the apartments to have a toilet that flushes. Not so in the bush. In fact, there are many bush communities where nobody flushes the toilet. Also, you would expect to turn on a water faucet, and have quick access to hot and cold running water. Once again, this is not to be taken for granted in the Alaska bush. I know a fellow teacher who runs a water hose into the house once a week, and fills an indoor water tank to supply cold running water to his house. He doesn't have hot water at his house, although he has access to a hot shower at school.

The absence of a flush toilet and hot and cold running water in your teacher housing might be a deal-breaker for you, or it might not be. Some teachers are perfectly happy using an incinerator toilet, a composting toilet, or a honey bucket. (You can search all of these terms on the Internet.) Taking a hot shower at school is part of the morning routine for many bush teachers. And typically, these teachers pay lower monthly rents. Saving $100 per month in rent is the equivalent of making an extra $1,000 a year in salary. Once again, the choice is yours. However, make sure to ask about the plumbing in your teacher housing unit before accepting a teaching position. You really don't want to find out that your toilet is really a plastic bucket on move-in day.

Are Utilities Included?

In some cases, teacher housing rental payments include utilities. Currently, Mrs. Rose and I pay $700 per month in rent for a small two-bedroom, one-bath furnished house with running water and modern plumbing. The rent includes our water, sewer, electricity, propane (for the cooking stove) and diesel fuel (for the heater and hot water heater.) The only household bill we pay is for Internet, which is part of our cell phone bill. (Landline phone and satellite TV service are available, but we choose to have neither.) Utilities are expensive in the bush, so our rent is a real bargain, especially during the winter months.

Find out if your utilities are included in your rental payments, and factor that into your job decision. Once again, don't be afraid to ask the interviewer direct questions about your housing.

Paying Rent

If the school district is your landlord, expect your monthly rent to be deducted from your paycheck. In most cases, the deduction is made pre-tax, which works in your favor. In other words, you won't have to pay payroll deduction taxes on the part of your salary that goes for rent. The tax savings can add up to several hundred dollars per year.

Location of Teacher Housing

Most villages build their teacher housing units right beside the school. While this makes perfect sense, it's not always possible. Some schools purchase existing houses in the village to provide teacher housing. Your teacher housing might be 20 steps from the school door, or it might be a mile or more. Once again, you need to determine the location of your teacher housing before accepting a position.

At first, the location of your housing might not seem that important. The villages are typically small, and walking a mile to school wouldn't be that bad, right? However, when the temperature goes below zero, the wind blows 30 miles per hour, and there's a sheet of ice on the road, you will not want to walk a mile to school. Teacher housing located more than a few yards from the school presents additional considerations.

Your teacher housing location will impact your lifestyle in ways you probably haven't thought about. If your teacher housing is close to the school, you can probably run home for lunch. Teachers living farther away won't have that option. Your teacher housing location can also dictate your clothing choices on cold days. The teacher living right beside the school can pull on a hoodie and trot to the school door. The teacher living farther away might need to "gear-up" with a parka, snow boots, and goggles for a long walk or ATV ride. Of course, living away from the school also has its advantages. Living in the village will help you make friends with the village residents, as opposed to contending with the isolation often felt by teachers living at the school site. Also, getting away from school lets you enjoy the village more. If you live on the school grounds, you can probably always think of a reason to stay at work a little later, or work all day on the weekends (which I don't recommend.)

Living away from the school probably means that you live closer to the village store and post office than your on-campus colleagues. Make sure to ask about your teacher housing location in relation to the village store and the post office. If you want to go to the store and pick-up a few items, how will you get there? Does the school have a van or an ATV that teachers can borrow? In some villages, the school is a mile or more from the village. When living in the bush, you will probably receive many parcels in the mail. How far will you live from the post office? Remember, very few villages in bush Alaska deliver mail to your door. Everyone has a post office box, and everyone goes to the post office to retrieve their mail. Perhaps the school has a system, where an employee drives the school minivan to the post office daily to collect teachers' mail and packages. Or, perhaps the post office is two miles away, and the school provides no such service. These are things you need to know before accepting a position. (If you find that you're "on your own" concerning transportation, you may need to buy an ATV to get around the village. Of course, this presents an additional expense, and is covered in Chapter 5: Getting Around.)

Washing Your Clothes

What provisions are made for washing and drying your clothes? Will your teacher housing unit have a washer and dryer? If not, will you have the opportunity to do your laundry at the school at night or on the weekend?

Can I Just Find a Place in the Village to Rent?

School districts that offer teacher housing typically require teachers to rent from them. If you have been to a village, you probably already understand that this is the correct decision. There is a housing shortage in many villages, and most villages would frown on a teacher occupying a house, thereby displacing a local family. In most cases, district-provided housing is a real bargain, and represents the upper-level of housing in the village. Recognize it for what it is – an incentive for teachers to accept the job at that school.

Districts that Don't Provide Teacher Housing

A few Alaska bush districts do not provide teacher housing. This is especially true for school districts with very few schools, and schools with very few teachers. Many Alaska bush schools have only one or two teachers, and the districts often provide a stipend for the teachers to rent in the community. Typically, an existing arrangement is in place with a landlord, and you can just move into the house vacated by the previous teacher. Once again, make sure you learn about your teacher housing before accepting the job.

Your housing will be an important element in your job satisfaction in the Alaska bush. Make sure to research carefully and ask lots of questions. When it comes to village housing, the best surprise is no surprise!

Uncle Wally's Tip: In the Alaska bush, water pipes occasionally freeze, despite our best preventative efforts. Always have a few gallons of water stored away to use until the pipes thaw. The Reliance Products Aqua-Tainer stores 7 gallons and is BPA – free (about $17 on Amazon.) When the pipes freeze and you're still able to brush your teeth, make some coffee, and take a bird bath, you'll thank Uncle Wally!

Chapter 2

You Need to Eat

Getting the food you need, and maybe the food you want

Like most things in bush Alaska, obtaining the food that you need is done just a little bit differently. But, with careful planning you can get all of the food items that you need, and many of the food items that you want. Let's look at navigating through your many choices so that you can get a good variety of nutritious foods for a reasonable price.

Before we get into shopping, let me emphasize the importance of eating healthy when you teach in the bush. Simply stated, healthy foods keep you healthy. If your body is healthy and filled with nutritious foods, you will be in much better defensive shape when the flu, colds, and other diseases start circulating the village and school. Thanks to God's grace and Mrs. Rose's efforts in providing nutritious foods for our household, I can say that I haven't taken a sick day all year!

When you read Chapter 4: Staying Healthy and Clean, you'll understand that health care is very limited in bush Alaska, and even your access to over-the-counter remedies will be limited. You don't want to get sick, if you can help it. Nobody should have to walk to work in zero-degree weather if they're not feeling well. Eating right is your number one strategy in staying healthy, and the importance of this is heightened in bush Alaska.

Bush Shopping:
How it used to be, and still is for
many Alaska bush teachers

I want to address the topic of "commando shopping" early in this chapter, because if you've read online forums or blogs about moving to the Alaska bush, you've probably encountered this concept. In an earlier era, bush teachers anticipated the food staples that they would need for the semester (flour, sugar, cornmeal, beans, rice, soup, freeze-dried foods, canned vegetables, etc.) and shopped in Anchorage for a few days before heading to the bush.

Typically, teachers would shop at Costco or Sam's Club all day, then spend the evening packing their supplies in plastic totes and heavy cardboard boxes. There's a post office near the Anchorage airport, so that would be the next stop. Of course, hotel rooms in Anchorage are very expensive in the summer, and some sort of vehicle is needed for the shopping trips and airport runs. After a day or two of commando shopping and shipping, the teacher would dump the contents of his suitcase into a cardboard box, ship it to his school site, and fill his luggage with frozen meat and perishable produce. Upon arrival at the village, the meat is tossed quickly into the freezer, and the produce refrigerated. About a week later, the totes and boxes of beans and rice start trickling in to the village post office. A similar return trip to Anchorage is planned for winter break.

Some teachers still do this. In fact, one school district that I know of (and probably a few others, too) meets their teachers in Anchorage, rents a van, and hosts a bush-shopping-and-shipping marathon! To these districts, I say "God Bless You!" They are going above and beyond to make sure that their teachers have the opportunity to shop. Some people actually love this type of shopping adventure. Mrs. Rose and I can't imagine doing this.

You don't have to shop commando-style. You simply need to plan ahead, and research vendors before you get to Alaska. (That's probably why you're reading this book!) In this chapter, we'll look at how the Rose family eats delicious and nutritious food in bush Alaska, without breaking the bank.

Three Thoughts Before We Shop

This section features some tough-love from Uncle Wally. Remember, I'm trying to help you, and it is better that you hear it from me now, than to realize it when you get to the bush. So, remember – this is for your own good.

#1 – Say Goodbye to Convenience Foods

If you've been a college student for the past four years, it's time to end your romance with convenience foods. Goodbye Hot Pockets. Hasta la vista frozen burritos. Arrivederci frozen pizza. Adieu Klondike Bar.

I'm sorry. I know that hurt. But somebody had to do it. The fact is, some foods are nearly impossible to obtain in the Alaska bush. Ironically, frozen foods are expensive and difficult to obtain in bush Alaska. And because of the distance between the food processing facility and your bush grocery store, I am very cautious about the safety of such food products.

Let me expand on that for a minute. For purposes of illustration, let's say that for you – living in the lower 48 - no morning is complete without a bacon, egg, and cheese Hot Pocket. That breakfast pastry delicacy was created in highly-controlled conditions in a food processing plant somewhere within driving distance of your home. It was packaged in sanitary conditions, stored for a brief period in a huge freezer, then loaded onto a freezer semi-truck. That truck was driven to your local supermarket, where trained workers immediately transferred the boxes into the grocery store's freezer. Within hours or days, the package of Hot Pockets appeared in a modern freezer case, and was probably purchased by you within a few days at most. You took the Hot Pockets home to your modern freezer, where they stayed until breakfast time.

You see the "chain of custody" there. Fast, frozen, nearby. Several people – from the worker at the food processing facility to the stocker at the grocery store – are responsible for making sure that you get a high-quality frozen Hot Pocket.

It doesn't work that way in the bush!

Please don't hold me to this, but I don't believe that we make Hot Pockets or frozen burritos or Klondike Bars in Alaska. Those items, and many more come from the lower-48 on an airplane. And it probably takes at least two more airplane trips to get to your village. Seattle to

Anchorage. Anchorage to Bethel or Dillingham or Nome. To your village on a bush plane. To your village store on a cart attached to the back of an ATV.

Now, please, please, please don't get me wrong. I'm not in any way criticizing anyone else's hard work in their attempts to provide food to the villages. I especially applaud the small village stores that do wonderful work in very difficult situations (as explained later in this chapter.) But when it comes to perishable items – milk, meat, eggs, produce, etc. as well as all frozen foods – if I can't reasonably understand the conditions in which that food has made its way to my village, then I don't feel safe eating it. Period. And Uncle Wally's advice is to avoid such situations.

#2 – Learn to Cook – at least a little bit

In most (if not all) bush villages, you won't have the opportunity to "grab something" on the way home. There are no pizza parlors or Chinese food take-out stands. If you want to eat a meal, you will probably have to prepare it. So, you need to learn to cook, a least a little bit.

Maybe you're already an accomplished cook. Or, maybe you just haven't developed that skill yet. Either way, your life will be easier if you learn to transform a few ingredients into a meal.

There are many cookbooks out there, designed for the new cook, the single person, and people who don't have a lot of time for meal preparation. I'm sure if you spend a few minutes on Amazon.com, you'll be able to find two or three cookbooks to get you started. Of course, the Internet is also a wealth of information for cooking simple meals. You can probably find a recipe app as well.

The important thing to remember is to keep it simple. You can start with dishes like stew, spaghetti, and baked-potatoes topped with chili. And as long as you're cooking, make enough for two or three meals. Plastic storage containers can hold the leftovers.

Mrs. Rose offers her "Northern Lights Soup" recipe at the end of this chapter. Make sure to check it out!

#3 – Prioritize Your Wants and Needs

Most of us learned about the major food groups in school, and certainly you want to have a balanced diet. Just make sure that your happiness doesn't hinge on your ability to get certain foods. I grew up in the southeastern United States, where fruits and vegetables are plentiful and inexpensive. I am used to watermelon, cantaloupe, and bananas in my refrigerator. Our village store got some small watermelons last August. They were $20! The bananas that I can buy in the bush are typically riper than I'm used to, and the one cantaloupe that I bought on a trip to Bethel was mushy inside. So basically, I just need to deal with it. Apples, and (surprisingly) oranges are relatively inexpensive here, so that's what we eat.

The same holds true with the brand names and processed foods that you may be used to. Yes, I can buy potato chips in the village store. The regular bag that would cost about $3 in the lower 48 sells for about $8 in a bush village. Okay – so I could buy a bag a week, and that would still be only $32 a month. You might choose to buy these items, but I can do without potato chips. It's a personal choice. But it is important to understand that you really don't have to have those things.

Buying Your Food

Living in the lower 48, you probably buy most of your food from one place – the grocery store. You might stop by a produce stand or the health food store for a few items, but recently most grocery stores have begun to carry those specialty items, too.

When you live in the bush, you will likely obtain your food from a number of different sources. They include:

Online ordering,
Bush shopping services,
Specialty vendors,
Your village store,
Friends back home,
Trips to a hub city,
Your village resources.

Of course, some of these overlap, so don't get too concerned over categories. Let's take a look at the opportunities that you will have when living in the bush.

Online ordering

You can find many food items for sale online. Surprisingly, many of the prices are actually lower than the grocery store prices in the lower 48.

Amazon.com carries a surprisingly wide variety of dry goods and canned goods. Among the items we buy from Amazon.com are: dried beans, oatmeal (instant and regular), canned chili, microwave popcorn, tea, dried fruit (raisins, apricots, etc.), dry pasta, peanut butter, and dried vegetables. An Amazon Prime membership is definitely worth the yearly $79 cost when you live in the bush. Amazon doesn't promise 2-day shipping up here, but we can usually get an order in a week or so.

If you see an item that you would like on Amazon (for example a certain type of canned soup) but it costs more than you want to pay, put it on your Wish List. Amazon will e-mail you when the price drops. And typically, the price drops, based on supply and demand. Amazon really isn't interested in a warehouse full of overpriced soup. Trust me, this works!

We also buy food from Swanson Health Products, an online vitamin and health food vendor. From Swanson we buy all-natural cup-a-soups, spices, pasta, cooking oil, and canned tomatoes. If you sign-up for the Swanson e-mail, you'll regularly have a %-off coupon code. Swanson has free shipping if you spend a certain amount (typically $50,) but they tack-on an extra $4 Alaska shipping charge. Still, that's a bargain. Swanson's prices are usually a bit below list price, the food is healthy, and the delivery is quick. Swanson Health Products is one of our favorite vendors. Some friends use Vitacost for similar purchases. I've never used Vitacost, but the people up here who use it report that they are satisfied.

Before we leave this section on online food ordering, let me make three important points. First, the shipping costs will play a big role in your food cost. Amazon and Swanson shipping charges are negligible. Other online vendors charge shipping costs that can double the price of your groceries. Shop around, and network with your fellow teachers. You're certainly not the first person to buy groceries online! If you're filling-out your first order with an online vendor, put a few items in the cart, and type in your zip code. You will quickly discover the bush-friendliness of the vendor.

Here's the second point to consider: quoted shipping times are nearly meaningless out here, because the final leg of the trip is really out of the vendors' hands. In the bush, we don't get UPS or FedEx. We get the United States Postal Service. Trust me, I am thankful that Uncle Sam provides me with the same postal service that I got back home. But remember – that last trip from the regional hub to my village is made by a passenger bush-plane service on a contracted basis. Those planes are small, and there's only so much room for large boxes. The lessons here are (1) always buy ahead, and (2) don't get upset with Amazon or Swanson or any online vendor if your packages don't arrive when "promised." Chances are, those boxes are sitting in the bush airline storage room, waiting for space on a bush flight.

Finally, all of these online purchases need to be made with a credit card. Most bush teachers have a credit card issued by an airline, and they earn "miles" for each dollar spent. Over time, this can result in free or discounted airline tickets. Just a thought.

Bush Shopping Services

Although Amazon is very popular out here in rural Alaska, they certainly didn't invent shipping groceries to the villages. Several bush shopping companies have been providing this service for years. Span Alaska Sales and Mailbox Groceries Alaska are two popular bush shopping services. You can request catalogs or browse their web-sites and quickly get an idea of the items that they carry. Also, Wal-Mart, Sam's Club, and Fred Meyer have bush shipping departments. You can call them, tell them what you want, and they will ship it to you.

Of course, these companies are in business to make money, and you'll pay for this service. Expect an upcharge (maybe 25%) on the price of the groceries to cover shopping and packing, plus the shipping cost. Before the Internet, this was probably the best way to get many grocery items. But now, many online vendors offer food at grocery store prices with free or low-cost shipping. Mrs. Rose and I have never used these bush shopping services.

Specialty Vendors

There are several vendors that specialize in quickly shipping food items that Amazon doesn't sell to remote locations – fruits, vegetables, and meat.

Full Circle Farms ships organic produce from the state of Washington. You can sign-up for a free membership, and select the size of the box you want. Shipments occur weekly, and your shipping day is indicated on the web-site. Typically, the produce arrives one or two days after it is shipped. Each box is custom-packed for the customer. You can accept the default selection of produce, or customize your box. You can also skip shipments if you don't need any produce. If this sounds expensive – organic produce shipped next-day to Alaska-you're right. At the time of this writing, the smallest box (15-20 servings) shipped to my village is $56. You can decide if that's the best choice for you.

Mrs. Rose and I get our produce from Tim Meyers at Meyers Farm in Bethel. Tim grows vegetables in Bethel, and imports other produce. (You can learn about his industrious operation on his web-site, http://www.meyersfarm.net/) Tim's shipping operation isn't quite as sophisticated as Full Circle. Typically, I send Tim an e-mail, and ask what he has. He usually responds the same day. Mrs. Rose and I make our wish list, and I send Tim an e-mail with an amount limit – usually $80.

My credit card number is on file in his office. Tim fills a box with $60 worth of produce, drives it to the airport, and hands it off to the bush airline that serves my village. The other $20 pays the freight to get the box to me. People from the villages served by the Bethel airport can use Meyers Farm. If that's your destination, I would suggest giving Tim a try. We have always been pleased with our boxes of produce.

Frozen meat can also be shipped to many villages. Mrs. Rose and I use US Wellness Meats out of Missouri. They stock a wide-variety of all-natural beef, poultry, and lamb. We usually stick to the ground meat. They ship to the village next-day. The meat is frozen solid and packed in a foam cooler with blue ice. The cooler is shipped inside a cardboard shipping box. Tracking information is provided via e-mail, and our order usually arrives within 36 hours of shipment. All of our meat has been frozen solid when we unpacked it. As with most services of this sort, the meat is expensive. However, the shipping cost is built-in to the price. A small order fee is added, that probably covers the cost of the cooler, the blue ice, and the heavy duty box.

Some Alaska butcher shops also ship frozen meat to rural Alaska. Probably the best known is Mr. Prime Beef in Anchorage. They offer convenient variety packs designed to fill your freezer. Mr. Prime Beef doesn't make any all-natural claims, but I have talked to teachers who order, and they say the meat is very good.

If you decide to order produce and meat from these businesses, here are a couple of things to consider. First, ask the teachers at your school about their experiences with vendors. Your first order should probably be with a vendor with a track record for speedy delivery to your village. For some unexplained reason, some products arrive quickly in some villages, and much later in others. Although we have always received quick shipments from US Wellness Meats, a teacher in another village reports that his first order never arrived, and his second order arrived two weeks late (yuck!) Of course, US Wellness cheerfully refunded his money each time, but after the second order, they suggested he try another vendor. He placed an order with Mr. Prime Beef, and received the meat, frozen solid, two days later. Go figure.

Here's another consideration: let your airport agent know when you're expecting a next-day order of perishable items. Bush airports have at least one airport agent who is responsible for reserving seats on the bush planes, transferring the mail between the post office and the pilot, and accepting packages and freight items. When I am expecting an order from Meyers Farm or US Wellness Meats, I call our airport agent and let her know. When the item arrives, she calls me. Sometimes she delivers the box to our house or the school, and sometimes I go to the post office to pick it up. (I follow her lead on that one.) But, it is nice to have that communication.

Your Village Store

Most rural Alaska villages have a general store where you can buy dry food items, such as flour, sugar, coffee, and tea. Some stores also carry a small selection of produce (apples, onions, and potatoes are regularly featured) and dairy case items, such as cheese, and butter. Your village store could also have a frozen food section. Your store might also stock some of the following items:

> Snack foods and sodas,
> Toiletries, such as toothpaste and deodorant,

Over-the-counter medicine,
Paper items (toilet tissue, paper towels, etc.),
Socks and underwear,
ATV and snow machine motor oil and spare parts.

Your village store could also be the vendor for gasoline, diesel, propane, and fuel oil.

Did you notice my use of the words "might" and "could" in the previous paragraph? That's because the size and quality of the village stores, as well as the selection of goods offered for sale, varies greatly from village to village. The upper-end of the village store experience would be a store in the Alaska Consolidated (AC) chain. You can look online to see if your village has an AC store. Although smaller in size, the village AC store will likely regularly stock the grocery items that you would expect to find in a small-town grocery store.

Several villages that don't have an AC chain store have very nice independent stores. The store in our village is owned and operated by the tribal council, and they do a very good job of stocking and managing the store. We have all of the items described earlier in this section. Our village store is open from 9 to 5, six days a week. Our village store is about the size of a typical large convenience store I frequented in the lower 48.

Unfortunately, some villages don't have access to a store like ours. Many village stores are profit-based ventures, and they only stock what they can sell quickly. I visited one village store where about 75% of the shelf space was taken by snack food and soda. In some very small villages, the village store is actually someone's home. These "stores" are typically open for one or two hours a day. Once again, mostly snack foods are offered.

Although we have a fine store in our village, we don't "grocery shop" there. We try to buy organic and all-natural food, and our village store rarely stocks these items. We typically buy most of our food online. However, there are a few items that I regularly buy at the village store. They include:

Apples and oranges,
Potatoes and onions,
Cheese and butter,
Sugar,
Pilot Bread (like jumbo Ritz crackers),
Herbal tea,
An occasional candy bar,
Sweatshirts with our village name on them,
Gasoline and motor oil.

Just like Wal-Mart in the lower 48, the village store is typically a place where you can meet and greet friends in the village, and catch-up on the village news. In our village, the store is right next door to the post office. You can almost always find 5 or 6 ATVs parked outside, and several people milling about inside. Could you do your grocery shopping in a village store like the one in our village? Yes, you could. In fact, two of our teachers do most of their grocery shopping in our village store.

So, when comparing villages and evaluating job offers, ask about the village store. It's nice to be able to stop on your way home and buy a few apples, a pound of sugar, and a box of Pilot Bread.

Your Friends and Family Back Home

It's great if you have friends and family members back home who are willing to go to the grocery store for you, buy that hard-to-find item, and ship it to your village.

Obviously, this is not your main source for groceries, but it is nice to have someone who will help you in this way. Let me give you an example: coffee is very expensive in the bush. A common-brand package (Maxwell House, Folgers, etc.) easily sells for $12 or more. When we lived in the southeastern United States, we shopped at Publix Supermarkets, and I still have their app on my iPod Touch. When my coffee supply starts to run low, I check the sales at Publix. Usually within a week or two, an acceptable brand goes on sale – sometimes buy-one-get-one free. I send an email to my daughter in Florida, who buys 10 or 12 packages, boxes them up, and ships them to me in the bush (typically shipping cost would be about $15.) So, for around $50, I can have 12 packages shipped to my house, thanks to my daughter in the southeast.

You get the idea – this is probably something you would do for a few hard-to-get items. I have heard that most online vendors won't ship chocolate to Alaska. I've never tried, but it makes sense. That would definitely be a welcome item in most teachers' P.O boxes. Maybe you're already thinking of someone who could send you a box of your favorite groceries every now and then.

A Trip to a Larger Town or City

Depending on the village and district you select, you may have the opportunity to travel to a larger town or city to buy groceries. Because travel to and from a bush village can be expensive, you probably won't be able to financially justify a trip to the city just to shop. But, if you're going anyway, you might want to pick up a few items and bring them back with you.

Most airlines charge $20 or $25 for each bag you check on your flight, up to a 50-pound maximum. So, you could conceivably cram 50 pounds worth of groceries into a suitcase and check the food as baggage. This would probably be cheaper than shipping through the post office. And because the baggage will be there when you get off the airplane, it will be much quicker, too. Typically, teachers will throw a durable duffle bag into a hard-side suitcase when packing for travel. At the conclusion of the trip, the dirty clothes go into the duffle bag, and fresh produce and other hard-to-find items fill the suitcase.

Remember that the plane that takes you to your village will probably be a small bush plane, and there will probably be different luggage allowances. However, the smaller airlines in rural Alaska understand that residents usually buy things when they come to town. If they can't fit your purchases on the flight you travel on, they'll store them for you, and bring them on the next flight.

As you can imagine, this should be a supplemental way of getting groceries, not your main strategy. However, I know of at least one large rural school district that flies all beginning teachers to the district office three or four times before Christmas for in-service training. That's a great opportunity for teachers to do some shopping in a regional hub city.

Your Village Resources

If you're interested in teaching in rural Alaska, you've probably heard of subsistence living. United States federal law defines subsistence living as

"...(T)he customary and traditional uses by rural Alaska residents of wild, renewable resources for direct personal or family consumption as food, shelter, fuel, clothing, tools or transportation; for the making and selling of

handicraft articles out of nonedible by-products of fish and wildlife resources taken for personal or family consumption; and for the customary trade, barter or sharing for personal or family consumption." ("BLM Alaska: Subsistence Program." BLM Alaska: Subsistence Program. N.p., n.d. Web. 16 Jan. 2014.)

Subsistence living is huge in Alaska, and many of the residents of your village will obtain most of their food by "living off the land." As a teacher, you may have the opportunity to participate in this practice, by catching, hunting, and gathering some of the food that you eat.

Here is something very, very important to understand about participating in the subsistence lifestyle: you need to have a native Alaskan village tribal member guide you through your first season of subsistence activities, and serve as an adviser any time you hunt, fish, or gather.

Basically stated – when you enter into the village as a teacher, unless you are a native Alaskan, you are an outsider. You simply should not expect to participate in subsistence activities without the full blessing of the elders.

The natural resources in Alaska – the water, the fish, the wild game, the berries – are considered community resources, to be shared by the community. You will see this when you move to the village. When a hunter kills a moose, the first cuts go to village elders who are not able to hunt for themselves. A substantial portion of the meat is shared with widows, family, and friends. This process is repeated, and everyone has enough food. The state limits the number of wild game animals (moose, caribou, etc.) that can be killed, and permits are required. Hunting is controlled by government regulations, and unwritten village practices. You need to make yourself aware of both categories before hunting, as well as local laws about gun ownership.

Fishing regulations are less strict, but you must be aware of the supply of fish and the needs of your village. Once again, the village elders are your best resource for this information. In many villages, the fish are plentiful, and you will certainly be welcome to catch all that you can eat. Other villages rely on seasonal salmon runs, which can vary from abundant to sparse. I know that you would not want to catch the fish that a village resident needs to feed his family.

Wild berries are abundant in most village communities, and there is certainly etiquette for berry picking. Understand that this etiquette is so natural to the village residents that they may not think to tell you, so you have to ask. One of the unwritten rules involves where you can berry-pick. The areas close to the village are typically reserved for the village elders. Younger gatherers who can walk farther should expect to gather berries from areas farther out. You also want to make sure that you aren't picking berries near someone's house. In the villages, housing lots are small and property lines are very fuzzy. But it is reasonable for someone to expect to gather the berries near their house.

If all of this sounds like a confusing dance, you're somewhat correct. That's why you need the constant advice of a tribal village resident. I have found that the maintenance workers at my school have been very valuable in their advice and guidance on these topics.

Before we leave this topic, be aware that the village economies are based more on goods than on currency. Village residents don't use money the way it is used in the lower 48. Many people do not hold jobs that pay a salary.

They work at subsistence living, providing food for their family. They add income with commercial fishing, craftwork, or other business endeavors. As a teacher, you will be in a currency-based economy. You will have the ability to buy the food you need. Your personal activities should be undertaken with this concept in mind.

Am I pulling the plug on subsistence activities by teachers? Absolutely not! Many teachers in rural Alaska hunt, fish, and gather on a regular basis. But they do so under the advice and guidance of village elders and residents. And if you find yourself in competition with tribal village residents in subsistence activities, you should step aside and allow the person practicing subsistence living to provide food for his family.

Our Food Ideas for You

Mrs. Rose and I brainstormed some quick topics about our food experiences in rural Alaska. Our ideas are listed in the paragraphs below.

Hot beverages

When we moved to Alaska from a much warmer climate, Mrs. Rose and I found ourselves drinking more hot beverages. For many years I've started my day with a few cups of coffee. I now enjoy hot tea (both "regular" and herbal) and hot cocoa. Put these "comfort drinks" on your list for rural Alaska.

Coffee

If you enjoy a cup of coffee in the morning (or any other time,) my advice is to buy coffee on-sale before you depart your home town, and ship it to yourself in the village. Coffee is very expensive in the village, and it's not much cheaper via online vendors. Most grocery stores have coffee on sale, sometimes buy-one-get-one-free. Sealed packages of coffee grounds stay fresh in the freezer. I currently have about 15 pounds of coffee on-hand.

Alcoholic beverages

Many rural Alaska communities are dry. In varying degrees, it is illegal to buy, consume or possess alcoholic beverage. Your school district will make you aware of these ordinances before you are hired. Violating these ordinances can result in legal charges, and will most definitely cost you your job and your Alaska teaching certificate. You can find a current list of dry communities by searching online: Alcoholic Beverage Control Board Dry/Damp Communities.

Milk

Some village stores – especially the AC chain stores – will stock fresh milk. Our village store does not. Honestly, I would be very hesitant to consume fresh milk in rural Alaska. Our store sells quarts of milk in sealed boxes for $4. That's too expensive for me. Granted, we're not milk drinkers. I add milk to my chai tea and hot cocoa. We have a large, re-sealable bag of Carnation instant milk that we ordered from Amazon. I typically mix a few ounces at a time in an empty peanut butter jar, and keep it in the refrigerator. (Instant milk tastes better after it sits in the refrigerator for a few hours.) If you really enjoy a glass of cold milk, you will probably be able to buy some from the school cafeteria. Other than that, instant's the way to go, if you ask me.

Bread

Bread is pretty rare in rural Alaska villages. There is a Franz bakery in Anchorage, and that might be the only mass-producing bakery in the state (don't quote me on that.) Anyway, we certainly don't have a bakery within 400 miles of my village, and Franz bread is the only brand I've seen since I've been here. Our village store has bread occasionally. It is sold from the refrigerator case. A loaf of sandwich bread sells for about $5. I think the multi-grain bread is $7. I'm not sure how many people buy it at that price. A few weeks ago I bought three loaves for $3 each and put them in the freezer. (The "Best By" date on the wrapper had passed.) The school cafeteria serves sliced bread occasionally. I can't remember the last time I saw anyone eat a sandwich in the village.

Of course, there is one type of "bread" that is very popular in Alaska: Sailor Boy Pilot Bread. (Hooray, Pilot Bread!) Sailor Boy Pilot Bread holds a warm place in the hearts of rural Alaskans. Pilot Bread is basically a palm-sized Ritz cracker, but without the buttery taste. Round, unsalted, and well...hard! A two-pound box has about 40 crackers, and sells for about $8 in the village. They are quite rich, and have 100 calories each.

Every Alaskan has their favorite topping for Pilot Bread, but peanut butter is the #1 favorite. In fact, many school cafeterias in rural Alaska make Pilot Bread and peanut butter available to students and teachers throughout the day. Sailor Boy Pilot Bread is a cultural phenomenon. It is Alaska "soul food." Embrace your inner Alaskan, and pass the peanut butter.

Eggs

In our village, the store occasionally has fresh eggs. As you would imagine, they are very expensive, and are sometimes pretty close to their "use by" date. If your village has an AC store, you might get fresh eggs on a regular basis. We usually buy a couple of dozen eggs when we go to the city. We have a container of whole egg powder that we bought on Amazon that Mrs. Rose uses in recipes, and for the occasional scrambled egg breakfast. Eggs aren't a big part of our diet in the bush.

Mountain House Freeze Dried Food

If you enjoy camping trips, or you like to be prepared for emergencies, you are probably familiar with Mountain House freeze dried food. There are many brands of freeze dried and dehydrated food, but in my opinion Mountain House consistently has the highest quality and the best taste. Freeze dried entrees, vegetables, and fruits are available. Preparation is easy: just add hot water, wait a few minutes, and you're ready to eat!

Mountain House food comes in two container sizes: pouches and large #10 cans. The pouch typically contains an entrée, such as Rice & Chicken or Beef Stew, and makes two servings. Entrees, fruits, and vegetables are available in the large cans. The entrée cans have about ten servings, and the vegetable cans typically have about 20 servings.

You can find Mountain House food at camping stores, emergency preparedness web-sites, and of course, Amazon.com. If you want to sample some of the entrées, check the sporting goods department at your local Wal-Mart, or the camping department at REI. Mountain House has recently begun packaging 12 pouches in a plastic bucket. It's called the Just in Case bucket, and sells for around $60 at Amazon.com. That's $2.50 per serving – not bad for a delicious and nutritious entrée that you can prepare with hot water in just a few minutes.

Some people make Mountain House part of their regular meal rotation. It's that good. However, there's a big reason to keep a stock of freeze-dried food: you might need it. When the weather is bad, the bush planes don't fly. A supply order could be delayed several days until the planes fly again (and there's no guarantee that your food order will be on the first plane, or even the 10th plane.) The village store could be closed in extreme weather conditions. You need to rely on the food that you have in your house or apartment.

Okay, that last paragraph was a little dramatic. Your principal and your fellow teachers aren't going to let you starve. But you really don't want to be in a position to have to ask your friends for handouts, or beg the cafeteria manager for a can of school pork and beans, especially when there's a tasty alternative.

Uncle Wally's Tip: Buy a few pouches of Mountain House food and pack them in your suitcase, so that you'll have them when you arrive in the village. You'll have a lot to think about when you first arrive in the village. You will appreciate having a quick, nourishing meal that you can prepare in your teacher housing. (You can probably round-up a pot to boil water in!)

Dried Fruit and Dehydrated Vegetables

We keep a supply of dried fruit, and to a lesser extent dried vegetables, in our cupboard. Dried fruits that I enjoy include: raisins, apricots, dates, figs, and banana chips. We also have a large can of Mountain House freeze dried strawberries.

Amazon sells quart containers of Mother Earth Products dehydrated vegetables. We like the spinach, the bell peppers, and the tomatoes. We also purchased a large can of Mountain House freeze dried green beans, and they are very tasty. We use dehydrated vegetables as flavoring for soups, salads, and stir-fry dishes. Of course, these ingredients also increase the nutritional value of foods they are added to.

Good Ramen

You can search the Internet and quickly discover that the cheap Ramen really isn't very healthy to eat on a regular basis. But, you don't have to give-up the quick and tasty soup. Shop health food web-sites (such as Swanson Health Products and Vitacost) and you'll find healthy Ramen noodle cups, without the artificial flavorings and MSG. My favorite brand is Dr. McDougall's. Sure, it's more expensive than the ramen bricks from the grocery store, but it is certainly much better for you!

Spices

When you begin preparing your meals, you will find that spices can really liven-up beans, soups, and stews. Mrs. Rose's favorite cooking spices include: cinnamon, oregano, cayenne, cumin, Italian mixture, garlic and ginger. We also buy seasoning mixes from Swanson Health Products. If you find that an online vendor won't send your spice order to Alaska, it's probably because of the glass jar. Switch to the plastic containers, and the order will likely go through.

Wild Game

As a resident of rural Alaska, you will probably have the opportunity to enjoy some of the freshest fish and meat you've ever tasted. And of course, it is all wild-caught, minimally-processed, and organic. But be prepared to eat some animals that you've never eaten before! You will probably have the chance to eat some moose and caribou. If you live near salt water, you will get the chance to eat beluga, seal, and walrus, too!

This is actually a great honor, because when a hunter presents you with some meat, it doesn't just show his generosity. It lets you know that he sees you as a member of the community – a person who gets a share of the meat. (Although it usually goes unsaid, some villagers will give a welcomed newcomer the meat that they would have shared with a deceased loved one. This is a special honor for you.)

Think about it now. You don't want a shocked expression on your face when a neighbor offers you the meat of an animal that you more closely associate with the zoo than the dinner table. Your correct response is to enthusiastically thank the giver, say that you've heard about this, and you can't wait to try it. It is appropriate and flattering if you ask the hunter how he caught the animal, and where he had to travel to find it. The story is part of the gift. Also, ask the hunter how he likes to prepare the meat of this animal.

Take the meat home. Wash it thoroughly. Cut off enough to prepare for yourself that night, and freeze the rest. If you're at a loss for preparing the meat, then add it to soup or make a stir-fry. Make sure to thank the hunter the next time you see him, and tell him how you prepared and enjoyed the meat. And don't be surprised if you really like eating an animal you wouldn't have dreamed of eating a few months ago. Mrs. Rose makes a great seal stir-fry, and a delicious caribou stew!

Storage Containers and Freezer Bags

No discussion of food would be complete without ... left-overs! Pack or purchase online a few storage containers, and a supply of freezer bags. When you cook a meal, cook enough for two or three meals, and store the rest for another meal. You can probably get four or five meals from a salmon, and you need to be able to freeze and store what you can't immediately eat. Planning your food storage can cut down on cooking time, and prevent food from spoiling.

Planning Ahead

Your rural circumstances dictate that you keep more food on-hand than your would in the city or the suburbs. As I wrote earlier, the weather may shut down all supply planes for several days, several times a year. Sometimes the village store will completely run out of popular items (and of course their supply stream is dictated by the bush planes, too.) When buying groceries and provisions, think in terms of months, not weeks and days. If you're buying instant oatmeal, peanut butter or microwave popcorn online, don't just buy a couple of boxes or jars. Estimate how much you will use in three months, and buy that amount. If you find you have more than you really need, you can always trade or share with your fellow teachers.

Have Some Food Waiting for You

In Chapter 8: Bringing Your Stuff, you'll find my advice about shipping your belongings to your village. Soon after you're hired, ask your principal about sending packages to the school, or to your teacher housing unit. He or she can provide you with a good address for shipping. Although the teachers and principal will probably leave the village over the summer, the maintenance workers – typically village residents – will be there to receive your packages, and take them to your housing unit. We were so thankful and relieved when we stepped into our teacher housing unit and found all of the boxes and totes we had shipped, as well as our grocery and household items from Amazon and Swanson Health Products were there. Of course, we placed a few more orders soon after, but we had enough to get us started. If you order your dry food items around the first of July, they should be waiting for you when you arrive at your site in early August.

Reimbursement

Some school districts reimburse their new teachers up to $1,000 for moving expenses. Your plane ticket and shipping costs will probably take most of that. But make sure to save your food receipts as well. Some school districts consider stocking the cupboard as an expense associated with moving. Ask your new district about moving expenses, and exactly what's covered.

What's In Our Cupboards, Refrigerator, and Freezer

Mrs. Rose and I have decided to let you take a peek into our cupboards, our refrigerator, and our freezer to get a good idea of what we keep on-hand. (I'm also including the items we have on-order.) We won't get into quantities or prices, but we will tell you what we have, and how we obtained it. As with the entire book, it is our goal here to provide helpful information, and give you some things to consider.

In the Cupboards

Peanut butter (Amazon.com)

Honey (Swanson Health Products)

Dried fruit: raisins, banana chips, apricots, figs, dates (Amazon.com)

Dried spinach, bell peppers, and tomatoes (Amazon.com)

Dehydrated hash brown potatoes (Amazon.com)

Mountain House entrees, green beans, and strawberries (Amazon.com)

Egg powder (Amazon.com)

Dry milk powder (Amazon.com)

Soup – ramen and noodle soup-in-a-cup (Swanson Health Products)

Olive oil (Swanson Health Products)

Dry pasta – various types (Swanson Health Products)

Brown rice (Swanson Health Products)

Dry beans (lentils, kidney, pinto, lima, white, black, garbanzo) (Amazon.com)

Yellow corn grits (polenta) (Amazon.com)

Oats (Amazon.com)

Instant oatmeal (Amazon.com)

Whole wheat flour (our village store)

Almonds (purchased on a "town" trip)

Microwave popcorn (Amazon.com)

Sailor Boy Pilot Bread (our village store)

Cocoa powder and carob powder (sent by someone in the lower 48)

Hot chocolate mix (Amazon.com)

Canned soup and chili (Amazon.com)

Vinegar (Swanson Health Products)

Herbal tea (Amazon.com)

Salt (our village store)

In the Refrigerator

Assorted vegetables (Meyers Farm, Bethel, Alaska)

Apples and oranges (our village store)

Eggs (purchased on a "town" trip)

Milk, made from dry milk powder (Amazon.com)

Cheese – cheddar, mozzarella (our village store)

Cheese – parmesan "sprinkle" cheese (our village store)

Bread (our village store)

Butter (our village store)

Coconut oil (Amazon.com)

Salad dressing (Amazon.com)

Sun butter (sunflower seed spread) (Swanson Health Products)

Crow berries (gathered by Mrs. Rose)

"Leftovers" (Mrs. Rose's excellent cooking!)

In the Freezer

Ground beef, chicken, turkey, and lamb (U.S. Wellness Meats)

Salmon (from village resident)

Halibut (from village resident)

Whitefish (from village resident)

Seal (from village resident)

Caribou (from village resident)

Crow berries (gathered by Mrs. Rose)

Ground coffee (sent by someone in the lower 48)

A Homemade Soup Recipe!

To conclude this chapter, Mrs. Rose agreed to share her method of making delicious soup. Enjoy!

Mrs. Rose's Northern Lights Soup

Select the dried beans that you would like to use for your soup for a total of one-half cup of beans.

Pour the beans in a bowl of tap water. Soak overnight.

Cut a medium-sized onion into strips, and place the strips in an electric crock pot. Add about a teaspoon of oil. Set the crock pot on low, and leave on overnight.

The next morning, drain the water from the beans, and rinse the beans with tap water. Place the beans in the crock pot with the onions.

Add 3 and one-half cups of water and one-half cup of brown rice to the crock pot.

Add additional ingredients to make your soup unique; these could include any combination of diced potatoes, diced sweet potatoes, sliced carrots, dehydrated spinach, dehydrated tomatoes, and dehydrated bell peppers.

Add meat if you choose. The meat should be pre-cooked before going into the crock pot. You can use ground meat, or chunks of local meat such as moose, caribou, or seal.

Spices can be added to change the taste of the soup. Adding a pinch of cumin and a pinch of cinnamon gives the soup a Mediterranean flavor. Add a little sweetener to create a Caribbean taste. Cilantro, cumin and a dash of cayenne will produce a southwestern flavor. Ginger, cumin, and garlic combine for an Asian flavor. Celery seed and rosemary creates a taste reminiscent of Thanksgiving dinner. Experiment with your favorite spices to create your own tastes.

Leave the crock pot on low, and let it cook several hours. (Crock pot times and temperatures vary, so be careful. Experiment on the weekend when you can monitor the cooking process the first time you make soup in your crock pot.)

When the soup is finished, reduce the crock pot setting from "low" to "warm." Enjoy your soup.

Refrigerate unused soup for future meals.

Chapter 3

Staying Warm and Dry

Clothes for living in Alaska

Another important consideration when moving to Alaska is your clothing – what to bring, what to buy, and what to wear. In this chapter, we'll take a look at clothing for the Alaska bush teacher.

Are you from Michigan, Wisconsin, or Minnesota? Do you spend your winters hiking in Maine, or snowshoeing in Montana? If so, you might already have a good idea of the clothes you need. There are a few unique considerations for Alaska, especially in the winter. So, I hope even you cold weather experts can benefit from reading this chapter.

Some Important Considerations

Before we get into specific clothing and vendors, let's look at some things to consider as you prepare your clothing choices for teaching in Alaska.

How much time do you intend to spend outside each day?

Some teachers come to Alaska dreaming about spending as much time as possible in the outdoors. Other teachers would rather make a quick sprint from teacher housing to their classroom. Of course, most teachers fit somewhere in between. You need to think about how much time you plan to spend outside.

Your teacher housing assignment can play a big role in the amount of time you spend outside. Here's an example: Teacher A lives in a teacher housing unit on the school grounds. The front door of her duplex is about 50 feet from the front door of the school. Each morning she steps outside her front door, and in 30 seconds she's entering the school building. Teacher B lives in a teacher housing unit that the school owns in the center of the village, a little more than a mile from the school. Each morning, he walks out of his front door and straps his backpack onto an ATV. He drives the ATV (which is a 4-wheeled motorcycle, if you didn't already know) through the village, and parks it next to the school. He covers the ATV handlebars so the controls don't freeze during the day, and walks in the school front door. This entire process takes about 25 minutes.

So, Teacher A takes a 30-second walk from building to building. Teacher B's commute takes about 25 minutes, including parking lot times. You've probably determined where I'm going with this: their clothing needs are different. Unless the weather is absolutely terrible, Teacher A could probably get by with a coat, a hat, and some light-duty boots. Teacher B will need a parka, rain pants, goggles, gloves, snow boots, and an insulated hat. This is just another reason to find out about your teacher housing assignment before heading north.

Additionally, your clothing purchases should reflect your planned recreational activities. If you plan on hiking, snowshoeing, fishing, or another similar activity, you will need the appropriate clothes. And my opinion is that if you decide to be a couch potato, you'll be missing the beauty of Alaska.

You will be indoors most of the day.

Because of your work schedule (and your sleep schedule,) most of your time will be spent indoors. Remember this when buying your clothes. Your housing unit and your school will probably be around 68-degrees at all times. Yes, it might be 10 degrees outside, but you won't be standing out in it! Inside your home, you will probably wear what you wear now in the lower-48. The same holds true for your work clothing. You may be tempted to buy several heavyweight wool sweaters for your teaching job. But unless you're teaching outdoors, you really won't need heavy clothing for your work day. I wear a parka to work, but I don't wear it while I teach!

Realize that as a teacher your clothing needs and work environment will be different from many of the residents of your village. They may be commercial fisherman, maintenance workers, or village police officers. They will work outside much of the day, or at least go out into the weather frequently. They will probably wear insulated bib overalls and heavy duty parkas most of the day. Be aware of this difference when you ask for clothing advice from the locals.

Alaska bush clothing is decidedly informal and rugged.

My first year up here, I planned to wear khaki pants and a button-up shirt to work every day. That lasted about three days. Since then, it has been blue jeans all day, every day. Daily clothing in Alaska is rugged, utilitarian, and decidedly informal. There is mud, rain, and/or snow most of the year. Don't plan to wear clothes that are delicate to the touch, and hard to maintain. If in doubt, ask your principal when you take the job. Later in this chapter, I'll write about my daily clothing. But for now, think informal and tough, from head to toe.

Don't count on buying clothes in the village.

Your village store may have a few items, such as gloves, socks, and hats. Other than that, don't plan to buy your clothing in your village. Most village stores can't afford to stock such clothing items in a variety of sizes. You will either bring your clothing, or purchase it online once you get to the village. Later in this chapter, you can read about my favorite online vendors.

What I Wear to Work Each Day

Here is what I wear to work each day. Your village may be different, and you can ask the principal when you take the job. You can probably ask your principal for the e-mail addresses of your future fellow-teachers, and they will help in this area.

Shirts   I wear a medium-weight short-sleeved or long-sleeved t-shirt. Over that, I typically wear a sweatshirt, a zip-up fleece jacket, or a rugged button-up shirt (canvas or chamois.)

Pants   I wear jeans, every day. To be more specific, I wear Wrangler Five-Star, because they are durable, roomy and cheap. My principal wears the same thing.

<u>Shoes and socks</u>   My favorite shoes are my Carolina boots. They are brown leather, waterproof, and are about ankle-height. I keep a pair of Cabelas leather low-hikers (brown, waterproof) at school, and I change into those when I wear my snow boots to work. I wear wool socks every day, because they are warm. I like the REI brand and the Cabelas brand.

The men I work with all basically wear the same thing. The ladies' clothing reflects a little more personal style, as you would imagine. However, the concept is the same: casual and rugged. Sometimes the ladies I work with dress-up a little nicer. We guys never do. Go figure.

The Concept of Layers

If you're from a northern climate, you probably know all about dressing in layers. If, like me, you're from the south, dressing in layers probably means wearing a sweater when it's chilly. If you're not familiar with dressing in layers, let me give you the run-down. Remember, this is clothing for a typical outdoor day, not a strenuous physical work-out. If you're looking for layering techniques for outdoor expeditions, check the REI website.

Your first layer, next to your body, is your <u>base layer</u>. Your base layer should be comfortable, and have the ability to wick or draw moisture away from your body. Some people like a polyester blend, but I prefer a cotton T-shirt. I buy a T-shirt a little thicker than the standard weight. My personal favorites are Champion, Wolverine and Dickies.

The layer on top of your base layer is your <u>middle layer</u>, and it's designed for insulation. Sweatshirts and zip-up fleece jackets work great for this layer. So do wool sweaters. If you want to get a little fancy, try a button-up canvas or chamois shirt.

The top layer is the <u>shell layer</u>. This is the layer that protects you from the weather. In the late summer or early fall in Alaska, the shell layer could be a lightweight waterproof jacket. Later-year choices could include a waterproof and windproof polyester softshell jacket, or an insulated down parka.

So basically, I wear my base layer and my middle layer to teach in. The shell layer is the jacket that I wear to work.

Outerwear

When Alaska residents think about outerwear, this is what we're thinking about – clothing that will keep you warm and dry in less-than-perfect weather. As you read this section, remember the question that I wrote about earlier in this chapter: how much time do you plan to spend outside each day?

Before we look at the individual outerwear items that you'll need, let me tell you about the importance of buying quality outerwear. Simply stated, you get what you pay for. Yes, you can find some bargains out there, especially if you don't mind "last year's color" or a previous version of an updated parka. But don't expect to find this gear in the discount store. You will need to shop at retail stores or online with companies that specialize in this kind of outerwear. (Shopping options will be discussed later in this chapter.)

It is never too early to start learning about the outerwear you will need. As you educate yourself, you will begin to recognize some of the leading outerwear manufacturers, such as Mountain Hardwear, Outdoor Research, The North Face, Columbia, and Marmot. You can read reviews online, and make some notes. You will pay a little more for these premium brands, but you will be glad that you purchased quality, durable outerwear.

Jackets, coats, parkas

My advice is that you will need three jackets to get through the Alaska winter: a waterproof rain jacket, a waterproof and wind-proof/resistant mid-weight coat, and an insulated parka. Remember, these jackets are worn over your base layer, and your middle layer.

Rain jacket

You will probably wear your rain jacket when you arrive in your village in August. The weather here in Alaska can change very quickly, and you always want to have your rain jacket with you. The rain jacket has no insulation. Its task it to keep the other layers from getting wet.

Before we go any further, let's make sure we know the difference between water-resistant and waterproof jackets. Rain will typically roll-off a water-resistant jacket in a drizzle or light rain. If you're running from the car to Starbucks to pick up a latte', then a water-resistant jacket will be fine. Of course here in the bush, we don't have cars, and we don't have Starbucks. So – it follows that we don't need a water-resistant jacket either! You need a waterproof jacket. Period. Don't compromise on this. If you're out in the rain for more than a few minutes in a water-resistant jacket, you will get wet! The rain will soak through the water-resistant material, and seep through the seams. Water will not soak through a waterproof jacket. The seams are taped, meaning a thin strip of plastic is attached to the back side of every seam. If you've ever bought a nice camping tent, you're familiar with this concept.

So, in Alaska, your rain jacket should be waterproof. You should expect to pay around $40 or $50 for a waterproof rain jacket.

Mid-weight coat

When the weather gets a little cooler, you're going to want a rain jacket with a little insulation. That's where the mid-weight coat comes in handy. Like the rain jacket, the mid-weight coat needs to be waterproof. There should also be some degree of wind-proofing or wind resistance. Depending on your location, the wind can blow 40 miles per hour or more. On a 30-degree day, the wind-proof/wind resistant feature makes a big difference. A hood is a nice feature to have on a mid-weight coat. Remember, you want some insulation in this coat. It doesn't have to be goose down or high-tech down substitute, but it does have to have insulating properties. This would be your typical "winter coat" in many places in the lower 48. In fact, when I lived in the southeast, this was the heaviest type of coat that I needed. An insulated, water-proof, wind resistant mid-weight coat will probably cost around $70 - $80.

Parka

If you live in rural Alaska, and you plan to spend any time at all outdoors, you will need a parka. A parka is a heavily-insulated winter coat with a hood. The parka typically extends below your bottom, and closes securely. The parka is designed to insulate your torso against the elements. Most parkas have Velcro cuffs that can be tightened around your wrists, and a draw-cord at the bottom to seal-out drafts. The parka typically has a cloth strip behind the zipper. Yes, frigid air can blow in through a closed zipper!

Your parka's insulation will be either down (from geese and/or ducks) or synthetic fiber. Some parka companies use a combination of both. I prefer down, because it is so warm, but some people swear by the synthetic fiber fill. Really, if you buy a quality parka from a leading manufacturer, either is fine. Down is rated by its "fill power." For Alaska, you'll want a parka with a fill power rating of at least 600. The REI web-site has a great section on fill power, and down vs. fiber fill.

Your parka also needs to be waterproof. This is the coat you will wear when its 10 degrees below zero (or colder,) the wind is blowing, and the snow is falling. Believe it or not, if you have on a good base layer, an insulating middle layer, and an insulated parka, your torso will be warm in these conditions. A quality parka will cost between $170 and $200. This might be the most expensive coat you ever own – but on the first frigid day, you'll be glad you have it.

Of course, there are other parts of your body besides your torso, so let's continue.

Snowpants/snowbibs, rain pants, and thermal underwear

You will also need some outerwear for your legs. Depending on the weather or your personal preferences, you have some choices.

Snow pants and snowbibs

Snow pants and snowbibs (overalls) are insulated pants that will keep your legs warm in an Alaska winter. Like your parka, your snow pants or snowbibs should be waterproof and durable. Some people wear these insulated pants almost every day, and some people wear them rarely, opting for thermal underwear under jeans instead. It's really a personal preference. I would suggest buying these after you get to the village. We don't live in the coldest of Alaska climates, and I don't wear my snowbibs very often. If I lived on the North Slope, I would probably feel differently. A good pair of insulated snow pants will cost at least $75. Snowbibs are usually a little more expensive.

Rain pants

You might decide against buying snowbibs until winter, but you will need some rain pants when you arrive in Alaska. This is the "pants" version of your rain jacket. Your rain pants need to be waterproof, with taped seams. Don't settle for water-resistant rain pants. Make sure your rain pants have wide pants-leg openings, so that you can put the pants on and remove them without taking off your boots. Rain pants that fold-up into a built-in stuff bag are easily stored in your school backpack. When buying your rain pants, you will probably want to buy a size larger than your regular pants size, so they will easily fit over your jeans. A good pair of waterproof rain pants will cost around $35.

Thermal underwear

Thermal underwear bottoms (long johns) will certainly keep you warm on a cold, windy day. It's smart to wear a pair when you want to go for an ATV ride or a hike in the winter. You will certainly want some extra insulation.

However, when you're talking about a short ride or walk to work, that's a different set of circumstances. Do you want the insulation under your jeans (thermal underwear,) or over your jeans (snow pants?) Personally, I prefer a pair of rain pants or snow pants, which I can take off when I get to work. Remember, your school will be cozy and warm, and you will probably want to take off the thermal underwear when you get to work. But, if you plan for some extended outings on cold days, you will want at least one pair of thermal underwear bottoms. Thermal underwear bottoms can be purchased for about $15 per pair.

Keeping the Head and Neck Warm

You want to keep your head and neck warm when you go out. Just like you wouldn't go out in the Alaska winter with short pants and a t-shirt, you wouldn't go out without insulation for your head and neck area.

Hats are not optional in rural Alaska. Unless you have a very thick head of hair, and you're really used to the cold weather, you will want to wear a hat almost every time you step outside. Here are some hats that you will want to own.

Baseball cap

Before leaving your home in the lower 48, toss a couple of baseball caps in the suitcase. When you arrive in the village and the weather is relatively warm, a baseball cap is the perfect head covering. Baseball caps are also great conversation starters. From my experience, rural Alaskans can be big sports fans (my village cheers for the Seattle Seahawks) and a cap from your favorite team will give your fellow teachers and the village residents something to ask you about, and something to remember about you. I am from the southeast, and a big Atlanta Braves fan. The first few weeks I was in the village, I wore my Braves cap everywhere. Village residents would say, "Here comes the Braves fan," when I walked into the store or post office. To this day, people ask me how the Braves are doing. Your local discount store sells baseball caps for less than $10.

Knit cap

Call it what you will – a stocking cap, a watch cap, a toboggan – the knit cap is an important item in your outerwear wardrobe. You will find that more expensive knit caps really insulate better than the cheap ones from the discount stores. (Carhartt is the brand of choice in my village, probably because that's the brand available in the village store.) Of course, knit caps are very popular these days, and you can buy them in a variety of patterns and colors. Many village residents hand-knit these caps, and offer them for sale in the village store. You might even be able to custom-order a knit cap in your village. Expect to pay around $10 for a decent knit cap. Hand-knit caps in the village are typically $25.

Insulated hat or fur hat

Depending on how cold-natured you are, and how much (or how little) hair you have, you might want to buy an insulated hat. There are many styles. I have a "bomber" style hat made of insulated nylon, with rabbit fur lining on the headband and earflaps. The flaps fasten underneath my chin. This hat is waterproof, and keeps my head warm and dry in the Alaska winter. You can expect to pay about $35 for an insulated hat with fur trim.

Many of the village women are skilled at the art of making fur hats. They make beautiful hand-sewn hats out of beaver and seal fur. These hats are typically very warm, and they are true treasures of the Alaska bush. Mrs. Rose tells me that I should buy one, and I probably will before the end of the winter. Expect to pay about $200 for a hand-made fur hat.

Balaclava

A balaclava is a head covering that, when fully extended, covers the entire head and neck, with the exception of the upper nose and eye areas. Typically, the balaclava is made from the cotton-polyester fleece material, but cotton knit balaclavas are also available. Your balaclava is a very flexible outerwear item. You can cover most of your face, or pull the opening down below your chin. I wear my balaclava underneath my insulated hat. A fleece balaclava can be purchased for around $10.

Neck gaiter

A neck gaiter is a tube of cotton or fleece material that covers your neck. These are very useful, especially when walking in the wind or riding an ATV. They are very inexpensive – around $5 each. There's not much to them, but a neck gaiter can make a big difference on a windy day.

Headband/ear warmer/ear muffs

Mrs. Rose has several headbands (also known as ear warmers) that she enjoys wearing. Typically, they are fleece and available in a variety of colors. They are a bit wider than the typical headband hair accessory, and do a good job of keeping the ears warm. Men with a full head of hair can wear these as well. Expect to pay at least $4 or $5 for a simple headband/ear warmer. Those made of thicker material will be a bit more expensive.

Some people also enjoy ear muffs, which are thicker, structured ear coverings, held in place by a headband. The behind-the-neck ear muffs are popular, because they don't interfere with your hat. Expect to pay $10 for basic ear muffs.

Neoprene face half-mask

Neoprene masks that cover the lower half of the face are popular with snowmachine and ATV riders. They certainly knock-off the chill. Some people love them, while others prefer a fleece or cotton face covering. My advice is try before you buy. A neoprene face half-mask sells for around $15.

Goggles/sunglasses

If you expect to spend some time outdoors, you will probably want some inexpensive snow goggles. The wind kicks-up pretty good out here, and goggles will keep rain, snow, and other debris out of your eyes. Mrs. Rose and I each own a pair of goggles with fog-resistant lenses, for which we paid around $20. Serious skiers can spend $100 or more for their goggles, but we are happy with our economical purchase. You can select from a variety of tinted lenses, but we both chose the clear lenses.

Sometimes we like to ride our ATV in the late afternoon, and we didn't want to limit the amount of light our goggles let in.

On sunny days I wear a pair of wrap-around sunglasses instead of my goggles. They fit over my eyeglasses, but they aren't too big and bulky. If you don't wear glasses, you can probably find a smaller pair, but I definitely like the wrap-around style. The earpieces fit snugly above my ears, and I've never had them fly off while riding. I paid about $10 for these sunglasses on Amazon.com.

Keeping Your Hands Warm

When it gets cold, don't plan to go outside without your gloves on. Where you currently live, you might be okay just sticking your hands in your pockets, or wearing some inexpensive knit gloves. In Alaska, you need to make sure you have the right gloves to keep your hands warm. Icy cold hands can be very painful!

I have a pair of <u>lightweight gloves</u> that I wear in late summer and early fall. Carhartt is the brand name, and they are made of polyester and spandex. They are water-repellant, and have Velcro closures around the wrist. I paid around $20 for these gloves.

My <u>winter gloves</u> are leather and polyester, and filled with 650 goose down insulation. These gloves are windproof and waterproof. They extend about three inches beyond my wrists, and are fastened by a Velcro strap and sealed with a drawstring cord. I paid $60 for my winter gloves, and I feel like I got a real bargain.

Believe it or not, there are times when the winter gloves are not enough. Wool <u>glove liners</u> form an extra layer of insulation between your hands and your winter gloves. They are surprisingly inexpensive – about $5 – and make a big difference.

Village craftspeople make <u>fur mittens</u> from beaver and seal pelts. These mittens typically extend to the mid forearm, and are very warm. As you can imagine, they are also quite expensive. Handmade fur mittens cost $200 or more in the village. As with the handmade fur hats, fur mittens are true Alaskan treasures, and you may want to treat yourself to a pair if you plan to remain in Alaska for a few years.

While we're on the topic of mittens, be aware that some people really like gloves, and some people prefer mittens. This is a personal preference, and you just have to decide for yourself. Mitten wearers point to the extra warmth from fingers not separately exposed to the cold. People who like gloves usually can't stand the thought of their fingers enclosed inside a mitten! Alaskan's pride themselves on their individuality, and I wouldn't begin to tell you which to choose.

Shoes

Alaska shoes should be durable, rugged, and waterproof. You probably won't need dress shoes or sneakers in Alaska, although I guess some people try it. Shoes that aren't built for the mud and gravel roads will probably get ruined very quickly. Here are the shoes that Mrs. Rose and I have found useful here in rural Alaska.

Leather low-hikers

Catalogs call these shoes "walking shoes" or all-terrain shoes. They are basically a cross between a cross-training sneaker and a light hiking boot. They are nice enough to wear with khaki pants, should the need arise, and rugged enough to wear hiking around the village. A decent pair of waterproof leather low-hikers will cost around $100.

6" leather boots

These are the boots that I wear to work every day. They fit above the ankle, and are very comfortable. You can choose work boots, which will be a little bit heavier, and more structured, or hiking boots, which will be lighter and more flexible. (I prefer the work boots, and Mrs. Rose likes her hikers.) Either way, they need to be waterproof. These are the boots that can take-on mud puddles, light snowfalls, and berry picking trips on the tundra. Some boots offer the choice of steel toes, which add extra weight. The composite toe offers a much lighter option for those wanting a toe-protective shoe. Expect to pay around $125 for a nice pair of 6" leather boots.

Snow Boots

You will want some snow boots for the Alaska winter. Snow boots are typically 10 to 12 inches tall, and have a thick tread on the bottom outsole. They may be rubber, or a combination of rubber and polyester or suede.

Typically, snow boots lace-up, but some are pull-on. Lined snow boots are available, and provide an extra layer of warmth. Any time there's more than an inch or two of snow on the ground, you will want to wear your snow boots. Good snow boots are very comfortable, and some people wear theirs all day. I keep my low-hikers at school, and take off my snow boots when I get to my classroom. Prices for good snow boots start at around $75, and go up. Kamik, Ranger, and Columbia make excellent snow boots that are reasonably priced.

Many Alaskans prefer bunny boots to consumer-oriented snow boots. Bunny boots are solid white rubber lace-up boots, developed by the military in the Korean War. Bunny boots feature a thick layer of wool sandwiched in between two layers of rubber. A pair of thick wool socks completes the ensemble. A pair of new bunny boots will cost around $80. (If you prefer black boots, those are called "Mickey Mouse boots.") Mrs. Rose and I both wear snow boots, not bunny boots, but we know several Alaskans who are loyal bunny boot wearers.

Around-the-house shoes

In Alaska, people typically take off their "outdoor" shoes when they enter a house. For that reason, you will need some "around the house shoes." Typically house shoes or slippers worn in the lower 48 will meet this need, but my advice is to buy some house slippers with solid bottoms, in case you need to quickly step outside. Lining is also nice to keep your toes toasty at home. Expect to pay about $20 for a pair of house shoes.

Some people wear lined Crocs around the house, and they are a bit pricier. Mrs. Rose has a pair of Sloggers low rain shoes that she bought on Amazon for about $25. They are waterproof, comfortable, and fancy enough to wear outside, weather permitting.

Socks

Back in the lower 48, I bought my socks at K-mart, and paid about $2 per pair. They were cotton, had a little bit of cushion inside, and were perfectly suited for the warmer weather. Up here, socks are the first layer of insulation for your feet on a snowy day.

We take socks seriously in the Alaska bush. A good pair of Alaska outdoor socks has a high wool content. There's nothing quite like wool to keep your feet warm. I buy the store brand from REI or Cabelas when they're on sale. REI's Low Light Hiker Socks are 71% wool, and Cabelas Ultimate Lightweight Wool Socks are 78% wool. You can go with a thicker sock but these do just fine for me. They cost about $12 per pair, but are definitely worth it, and you can usually find them on sale.

Ice Cleats

Ice cleats are tire chains for your shoes. The chains attach to your shoes or boots using rubber straps. These chains give you more traction when walking on icy surfaces. You can find several brands online, at various prices. Read the descriptions and user reviews to determine which brand is best for you. Because you probably won't need ice cleats when you arrive in your village, you can ask your fellow teachers about their favorite brands. Make sure to have a pair when that first layer of ice forms on the ground. Ice cleats range in price from around $20 to around $50.

Bringing Your Outerwear vs. Buying It When You Get Here

This is a debate that rages among teachers and in online Alaska teacher forums: should you buy your outerwear before you come to Alaska and bring it with you, or should you wait until you arrive in the village and order what you need?

As you know, this book is all about giving you the information, and letting you decide for yourself. So, here's the information!

When you get here...

You will need a few items when your boots hit the ground in Alaska. And boots are at the top of the list! You will need some waterproof hiking boots when you get to your village. Village roads are gravel or dirt, and there are many potholes and mud puddles. Your new Air Jordans or Reebok running shoes will be soiled beyond recognition as you walk or ride from the airport to teacher housing. Buy some hiking boots, break them in before you leave home, and wear them to the village.

You will also need: jeans, t-shirts, sweatshirts/hoodies/sweaters, waterproof rain jacket, waterproof rain pants, lightweight gloves, wool socks, a knit cap, and a baseball cap. Depending on your "nature" and your acclimation to cooler weather, you may also want your medium-weight coat. Assuming you arrive in your village in early August, the weather will already be brisk, windy, and rainy. Using the layering approach, this clothing will probably get you through the first month. However, when you get your first paycheck, you need to plan to buy your cold weather gear. The cold weather will be coming, and Alaska has little sympathy for the unprepared!

Saving money by buying early

Your winter clothing – the parka, the insulated hats, the snow boots – will probably go on sale in the springtime. You can save some serious money by buying these items before you come to Alaska, if you're reasonably sure that you need them. For example, I saved $100 on my parka by buying it in April, before I came to Alaska. High-end outerwear manufacturers like to offer "updated" clothing each year, putting the previous year's items on deep discount. My parka is the Marmot Whitehorse, which Marmot doesn't make anymore. I'm okay with that – it's an outstanding parka, and we don't have many winter fashion shows out here! I'm happy to wear last year's parka, in last year's color scheme. If you're reasonably sure what you need, shop the close-out sales and buy early.

Another reason to buy in the lower 48 and ship to Alaska is the shipping cost. Many outerwear online vendors will ship free to the lower 48. But most of these companies add an additional Alaska shipping charge to your order. As you'll learn later in this book, you can ship a 40-pound tote to your village for around $40. Your mid-weight coat and parka will probably roll-up and fit in a corner of a shipping tote. Yes, you will have to pay to ship your coats to Alaska, but your shipping cost will probably be a lot less than the online vendor charges.

Once again, the key phrase is "if you know what you need." I had the benefit of Skyping with the principal and teachers at my Alaska school before moving up here. I asked bluntly: "Tell me, what do YOU wear?" They kindly obliged, and I was able to confidently buy what I needed.

Even if you plan to buy most of your outerwear before arriving in Alaska, expect to buy a few items as you need them. As the weather became colder, I realized that I needed some serious gloves, so I bought them in November. I ordered my snow boots about the same time. And I didn't think I would really need the wool socks my colleagues suggested, but I quickly realized that I needed to order them. So, you will certainly have the opportunity to buy clothes when you get here. Just realize that you can pay more in shipping charges, and you will probably have to wait an extra week for the items to arrive in your village.

Don't go on a shopping spree

You will probably be very excited about your move to rural Alaska, and you certainly want to be prepared for the weather. However, my advice is to resist the urge to go on a shopping spree.

I'm reminded of a new teacher I met a few months ago. She was lamenting the fact that before flying out to the village, she went to a nationally-known outdoor store, spent about $1,000, and didn't really get what she needed. Instead of buying jeans, sweatshirts, and wool socks, she bought clothes for an Alaska adventure expedition. I don't think the salesperson was trying to mislead her. We just need to remember that we're buying clothes to live out here. In all my time in Alaska, I have never hiked hours in the snow or camped-out on the tundra. I teach school in a modern classroom, walk around the village, and go berry picking occasionally. I don't need clothes for an Alaskan adventure. I need clothes for an Alaskan life.

"Fancy" is not the norm

In the Alaska bush, most people don't wear fancy clothes. It is perfectly fine if you have three or four pair of jeans, and three or four sweaters to wear to work underneath your coat or parka. No one is going to call attention to the fact that you've worn that outfit already this week. Neat and clean are important concepts. New and fashionable – not so much.

My Favorite Vendors

There aren't too many stores in rural Alaska that sell quality outerwear. Online shopping is the norm here in Alaska, and most teachers can tell you their favorite online vendors. Here are mine. (Realize that it's possible that these web-sites, business names and shipping policies have changed since this book was published, so always use your best judgment.)

Cabelas, the World's Foremost Outfitter, has a wide variety of cold-weather clothes, boots, and gear. Make sure to check the Bargain Cave for great deals. http://www.cabelas.com

REI is another great source for upper-level outdoor clothing and equipment. REI is designed more toward gear for outdoor activities, but you can still find almost everything that you need. A $20 lifetime membership (optional) gets you members-only discounts, special deals, and an annual 10% dividend refund on full priced purchases. The REI Outlet section of the web-site has great deals. Make sure to download the app, and check the Deal of the Day and Deal of the Week. http://www.rei.com

Most people are familiar with the Wrangler brand of jeans. Wrangler makes dozens of different types of jeans, and most stores don't carry them all. You can find all of the jeans that Wrangler makes in a large variety of sizes on their web-site. They also have shirts and jackets, as well as Big & Tall sizes. Make sure to check-out the Sale page on the web-site. http://www.wrangler.com

Sierra Trading Post is an enormous online store that features just about every type of clothing for men, women, and children. Sierra Trading Post specializes in closeouts and deep discounts that you can access through their e-mail list. Make sure to sign-up for that one. Their shipping prices are expensive to Alaska, but you can make-up the difference if you shop the sales. http://www.sierratradingpost.com

The Clymb sells outdoor clothing and gear at discount prices. You have to become a member (free) to shop there, by giving them your name and e-mail address. Discount codes, promotions, and sale notices will come to your e-mail box on a regular basis. The Clymb is more youth-oriented than some of the other online stores, but they had the best price on the gloves I wanted. Groovy! http://www.theclymb.com

There are many online shoe stores, but Shoeline.com is my favorite. They have good prices, free shipping, and a simple return process. http://www.shoeline.com

Most people who have purchased outdoor clothing or gear are familiar with The Sportsman's Guide. Their fun catalogs feature a wide range of items, from boots and clothes to housewares and ammo. Because The Sportsman's Guide features close-outs purchased from other stores and manufacturers, the selection can be hit-and-miss. Still, they maintain a surprisingly complete inventory of many of the clothing items Alaskans need. http://www.sportsmansguide.com

Hanes.com is a great place to shop online for your underwear and light socks. The Hanes web-site carries all of the products made by Hanes, so you can probably find what you need in your size. Shipping is a bit expensive, but sales and online coupons bring down the prices considerably. http://www.hanes.com

New York Lingerie is another great place to buy underwear online. They carry many of the popular brands, and their prices are usually well below suggested retail. They also carry shorts and t-shirts. http://www.nylingerie.com/

Yes, it's true – you can buy almost anything on Amazon.com, including clothing and shoes. Typically, I check all of my clothing, outerwear, and boot shopping against Amazon. Sometimes the Amazon price is lower, when you factor-in free or discounted shipping. http://www.amazon.com

Sign-up for e-mails and search for coupon codes

I've mentioned discount codes and special offers in the section above. My advice is to join the mailing list of your favorite online vendors. They all want customer loyalty, and one way they do that is to make sure their customers are getting their best prices. Some vendors send "members-only" e-mails daily, while others are less frequent. You can certainly save a lot of money this way.

If you don't have a current coupon code for your favorite vendor, search the Internet for one! For example, Google search for "Hanes.com coupon" and see what happens. Several web-sites regularly post the latest and most successful coupon codes for hundreds of online companies. If one coupon code doesn't work, try another! This is a great way to recoup the extra shipping costs you incur by living in Alaska.

If all of this sounds a bit nefarious – don't worry, it's not. Online companies are totally on-board with the coupon web-sites, often paying a small commission for all of the business the coupon web-site refers to them. If the online company didn't want you to use the coupon, they could easily block it. Remember, the coupon was their idea to begin with. Take the discount, smile, and maybe you'll become a loyal customer!

A caution about counterfeit clothing

Higher-end outdoor clothing items are among the most counterfeited items in the marketplace. One national news report claimed that up to 70% of outdoor clothing is counterfeit. So, how do you stay away from these bogus goods? Shop only from well-known, established, reputable businesses. It's hard to imagine verifying the authenticity of your clothing during an eBay purchase, or from a little-known online vendor whose address is a post office box or a suite number. Unless you get tremendously lucky at a thrift shop or garage sale, you're not going to find a 650 goose down North Face parka for $50. Be very cautious, and remember if a deal seems too good to be true, it probably is.

Uncle Wally's Tip: Always compare prices with two or more vendors. Put the item or items in the online shopping cart, enter the zip code, and compare the totals. Even with a discount code or special offer, you might be able to find a better deal on another reputable web-site.

As we close this chapter, let me encourage you to dress in Alaska to your personal comfort level. Don't compare your clothing needs to anyone else. When you move to rural Alaska, you will meet people who have lived here all of their lives. They may walk around the village in a sweatshirt, while you're bundled-up in your parka. That's fine. They are used to the weather, and you are not. The important thing is for you to be comfortable with your clothing. If you're cold, then put on an extra layer or a thicker jacket.

Remember, your clothing in Alaska – from hats to gloves to boots, from base layer to outer shell – needs to be rugged and durable. You need protection from the wind, the cold, the rain, and the snow. Make sure that you buy the clothes you need to be warm, dry, and comfortable as you live and work in Alaska.

Chapter 4

Staying Healthy and Clean

Taking care of yourself in the Alaska bush

If you've read this far, you're probably convinced that life in rural Alaska is quite different from life in the lower 48. One of the biggest differences is your access to medical care. Don't worry – bush Alaska residents can get medical care when they need it. But, just like most other areas of life, we have to do things a little bit differently out here. My hope is that this chapter will help you live a healthy and sanitary life in bush Alaska. It takes a little planning, but it can be done.

Many teachers I've spoken with say they feel healthier here in Alaska than they do in the lower 48. Typically, the air is fresher, the wild game and berries are organic, there is overall less pollution in the air, and there's not a lot of pollen flying around. So, let's be optimistic and say that if you follow the advice in this chapter, you'll certainly have good reason to feel better when you move to Alaska. That process begins before you arrive in the state.

Before Moving to Alaska

Many of the issues that could potentially negatively impact your health in Alaska can be prevented with a few tasks and lifestyle changes before you get here. If you've decided to move to rural Alaska, take care of the following items before you come.

Walk

You probably won't have access to a vehicle when you arrive in your village. You might be able to get an ATV ride from a fellow teacher, but honestly you don't want to have to depend on it. People in bush Alaska walk, and if you're going to live out here, you should get used to walking a mile or more without giving it another thought.

You might be an athlete already, and that's great. Many of us, through college or professional life, have become quite sedentary. If that's you, start walking! Take a brisk walk around the neighborhood or in a park every day. Take the stairs instead of the elevator. At the shopping plaza, walk from store to store instead of moving the car several times. (Of course, we want to be safe. We're all grown-ups here.)

Notice I didn't write "get in shape." If you're not in peak athletic condition, that's okay. Becoming physically fit is a lifestyle, and if you're not in top shape, it will likely take a few months or years of changed habits to get your body where you want it to be. But we're not talking about that. We're talking about the ability to walk a mile or more without getting out of breath. Start slowly if you need to. But start walking to condition yourself and build your stamina before you arrive in Alaska.

Note: Please understand that I am not saying that you must be physically able to walk a mile to teach in Alaska. Many people, because of physical disabilities and health issues, are unable to walk distances, and are still wonderful rural Alaska teachers. It is not my intention to discourage or belittle in any way. I'm really talking to people like myself, because I abandoned most strenuous physical activity during my college and early career years. And as always, consult your doctor before beginning any physical fitness activity.

Give up the junk food

Another way to prepare your body for moving to the Alaska bush is to give up the junk food. You probably won't be able to get those quick snacks in your village anyway (or if you do, they will be very expensive.) I'm not saying that you have to eat nuts and berries all day. Simply stop eating the sodium-filled, sugar-coated, dye-infused, artificially flavored convenience foods. You will feel much better, and you won't have to go through junk-food withdrawal when you enter the village.

Stop smoking and drinking alcohol

Wow, did I hit a nerve there? Maybe. But, as I wrote in Chapter 2, many/most rural Alaska villages are dry. In many villages, people in possession of alcohol can be arrested and hauled-off to jail in the regional hub city (where ironically, alcohol may be legal.) Your school district will probably educate you on this policy. I know I had to sign a sworn statement that I would abide by my village alcohol ordinances, or surrender my teaching certificate. If you're living in a dry village, you won't be able to drink alcohol, and you shouldn't expect otherwise. So – better to stop now, get it out of your system, and change your entire outlook on drinking alcohol.

Everyone knows the health risks of smoking, but some people still smoke anyway. Smoking is legal, and very expensive, in bush villages. However, most schools have vigorous programs to curtail the use of tobacco in all forms. Teachers are expected to model the behaviors that are expected of their students. Will smoking penalize you in the school setting or diminish your chances of getting a teaching job? Probably not. But understand that tobacco addiction is a social problem that most villages struggle with. As a teacher and role model, you should help your community as part of the solution to this problem.

Find a good multivitamin, and start taking it

I have taken a multivitamin each day for many years, and I firmly believe that it improves my overall health. Teacher-to-teacher, I would encourage you to do the same. The common argument against taking a multivitamin is that a well-balance diet filled with healthy foods from all food groups provides all of the vitamins and minerals a person needs. Of course, after reading Chapter 2, you understand that obtaining these foods, especially fruits and vegetables, can be a real challenge. A multivitamin can certainly help fill-in the gaps in your daily nutrition.

Finding the right multivitamin can be a task for some people. For years, every time I tried to take vitamins I would feel nauseous. My friends advised me to take a multivitamin on a full stomach, with a full glass of water, but that didn't help. Finally, I learned that many vitamins contain gelatin derived from beef or pork. Pork products disagree with my stomach, and I don't eat them to this day. With a little online research on the Swanson Health Products web-site, I found several multivitamins that have no meat, and that's what I use. They aren't more expensive or difficult to obtain. It just took a little effort on my part.

Visit a physician

Before moving to bush Alaska, visit the doctor's office for a check-up. This might sound overreaching, especially if you feel healthy. But, your access to a doctor will be limited for the next several months. If you have any health concerns or questions for a doctor, now is the time to ask them. You can also ask your doctor to recommend specific vitamins, as mentioned in the previous paragraphs. Explain to the doctor that you will be moving to a remote Alaskan village. He or she might be able to offer specific advice that will improve your health as you begin your new adventure.

Plan for prescription drug needs

You will not have face-to-face access to a pharmacist in a bush village. (Village health clinics, discussed later in this chapter, dispense medicine as needed to their patients.) If you take maintenance medications, or you have other prescription needs, make sure to talk to your doctor about this. In rural Alaska, most pharmacy needs are fulfilled via mail-order, and most school districts have prescription drug plans. Obtaining prescription drugs is certainly possible, but like many tasks in the bush, this task is accomplished with a little bit more planning, and a little bit more effort.

Visit the dentist

I won't make a checklist here. If you're old enough to teach school, then you know when you need to go to the dentist. Many people don't like dental visits, or the expense associated with dental work. My firm recommendation is to visit a dentist for a check-up, and get any dental work you need before heading out to the village.

In our village, the dentist comes three or four times each year, and stays about three days. He sets-up shop in the village health clinic, and sees patients continuously. For many village residents, this is their only dental care experience. In the lower 48, you likely have relatively easy access to dental care at any time. It doesn't make sense for you to take one of the traveling dentist's limited appointments, when you could have taken care of it back home. Yes, you can see the traveling dentist if you need to. But you will probably be much happier taking care of your dental needs before heading to the Alaska bush.

Dental emergencies in the bush are treatable, but they aren't pretty. The village health clinic can give you painkillers, but that's about it. You would need to take a flight to a regional hub, and sit in the dentist's office there until they can work you in. Sometimes the weather cancels flights for a few days at a time. Your school health insurance policy will probably include dental care, but it probably won't include the flight (and return flight) to the dentist, the hotel and food expense waiting to see the dentist, and the lost sick-leave used in such an episode. I don't mean to frighten you. Just understand that going to the dentist in the lower 48 is definitely preferable to a dental emergency in bush Alaska.

Visit the eye doctor

Eye exams in the lower 48 are convenient and inexpensive. You may even be able to get an eye exam as a walk-in patient at a national-chain eyewear store. If your vision prescription is a year or more old, or if you've never had a professional eye exam, I strongly encourage you to visit your optometrist before moving to the bush. If like me, you depend on eyeglasses daily, make sure that you bring a back-up pair to your village. If you wear contact lenses, arrive in the village with a supply, and establish an account with a mail-order contact lens vendor before leaving home.

The optometrist visits my village twice a year, sets-up shop in the village health clinic, and takes care of the vision needs of all of the village residents. He/she hands out prescriptions, but doesn't make eyeglasses. You want to take care of your eyeglass and contact lens needs before moving to the village.

But wait, won't I have insurance for that?

Good point. Your district will probably provide a fringe benefit package that includes dental and vision benefits. Why pay for something that you'll get for free in a few months?

It's all about access, and responsible planning. Where you live now, you might be able to get a new pair of glasses during your lunch break for a very reasonable price. Out here, that's not going to happen. Or your family friend the dentist has an office just down the street, and she'll be happy to work you in this afternoon. Once again, that's not happening out here. If you decide to fly to Anchorage or the lower 48 during the Christmas holidays, I encourage you to make dental and eye appointments if needed. If you need to visit your family doctor, make that appointment, too. Save your receipts, and get reimbursed by your school district when you return to the village. (Of course, you'll want to confirm your insurance benefits with the district office before running-up medical bills.) But when you make your first trip to the village, you want to make sure your immediate health, dental, and vision needs have been taken care of.

Health Care in the Village

In the paragraphs above, I've hinted about health care in the village. Let me do a better job of explaining it now.

In rural Alaska, a tribal health system serves the medical needs of Alaska bush residents. These tribal health systems are regional, and networked together by state-wide organizations. These systems provide excellent health care in environments that can be challenging and difficult.

The tribal health systems operate health clinics in most villages. Staffing of the clinics depends on the size of the village, and the available medical personnel. Most village health clinics will be operated by a Community Health Practitioner who has received extensive training in village health care. Some larger villages have a doctor, a nurse, or a nurse practitioner.

If this all sounds like "wild west medicine," it's not. The village health clinics have access to doctors via telephone and sometimes video-conferencing. Diagnostic equipment is available in many villages. Patients with medical needs beyond those that can be administered by the health clinic staff are evacuated via helicopter or airplane to the nearest hospital. If a specialist is required, the patient is flown to Fairbanks, Anchorage, or Juneau. (Typically, travel expenses are paid for a family escort as well.) A family friend who is a principal in the extreme northwestern part of the state experienced chest pains one morning. Within a few hours, he was having open-heart surgery in Anchorage. He recuperated fully in an

Anchorage extended care facility, and was able to return to work within a few weeks. People in rural Alaska take their health care seriously. But like many other aspects of life, it just looks a little bit different out here. Here's a web-site where you can learn more about specific healthcare in the villages you are considering: https://www.alaskatribalhealth.org/

Over-the-counter Medicine

You will probably want to keep an assortment of over-the-counter medicines in your rural Alaska home. You probably have some medicine in your home in the lower 48 now, but it is much more important here in the bush. First, your village store will probably have only a small selection of medicine, and may not have what you need. And like most store items, the prices will be very high. Some village stores – those run strictly for profit – may have no medicine at all. Secondly, even if your village store has what you need, it might not be open when you need it. Our village store closes promptly at 5:00pm each day, and isn't open on Sundays.

So, we might not have the selection we want, the price will be high, and unless we can schedule symptoms during the workday, it's all pretty meaningless anyway. Time to stock the medicine cabinet. Here are my suggestions.

Pain reliever, such as aspirin, Tylenol, Advil, etc.

Sinus headache medicine

Allergy medicine

Cold symptom medicine

Cough syrup and lozenges

Acid reducer

Antacid (sodium bicarbonate)

Bismuth tummy medicine (Pepto-Bismol, etc.)

Eye allergy drops

Wow, does that mean you can expect to be sick the whole time you're up here? No, not at all. It means that you're prepared, should sickness come your way. You don't want to spend the night with a tummy ache, waiting for the village store to open. You will also be the hero of your school when you can provide these remedies to a fellow faculty member who is not as prepared as you are.

Other Items for Your Medicine Cabinet

Cuts and Scrapes/minor injuries

Band-Aids

A couple of Ace bandages

Isopropyl alcohol. Believe it or not, isopropyl alcohol can be difficult to obtain in the village. It is highly flammable, and most vendors won't ship it. It is also heavy, relative to cost. Still, isopropyl alcohol is valuable for its disinfecting properties. As an alternative, you can order hand sanitizer, or packaged alcohol wipes.

Hydrogen peroxide. This is another cleansing, sanitizing solution. It is easier to buy online, but probably won't be available in the village store.

First-aid cream, such as Neosporin

Cotton swabs, and perhaps cotton balls

Foot care

Athletes foot cream (Clotrimazole Anti-Fungal Cream)

Foot powder

Dental Care

Four or five toothbrushes. I buy major brands from Dollar Tree in the lower 48. A toothbrush is $7 in my village store, and they don't always have them. Think of the admiration you will gain from your colleague when you can present him or her with a brand new toothbrush in the springtime!

Toothpaste. I use an all-natural toothpaste from Swanson Health Products. A medium-sized tube of toothpaste is $6 in my village store.

Dental floss

A tube of oral anesthetic gel, for minor tooth and gum pain

Buying These Items

You should buy most of the items above (notably, with the exception of the flammable items which should not be mailed) in your local drugstore or Dollar Tree in the lower 48, and ship them to yourself in the village. You can probably find most of the items on sale, so check the sales papers for Walgreens, CVS, and other drugstores.

You can probably fit your medicine cabinet supplies in a heavy-duty shoe box for mailing.

Soaps and Shampoos

Realize that your favorite brands of soap and shampoo will probably not be available in the village store, or they might be very expensive. I buy Clearly Natural Essentials soap which sells for about $1.50 a bar on the Swanson Health Products web-site. We also like Dr. Woods Pure Peppermint Castile Soap, which is an all-natural liquid soap. Thirty-two ounces cost about $6.50 from Swanson Health Products. I use this soap as shampoo, but with my hairstyle, I don't use a lot of shampoo.

If you use hair grooming supplies, you will want to find them online, and determine the cost effectiveness of buying them online, or buying them in the lower 48 before you come to the village. I will say that hairstyles in rural Alaska tend to be simple, and most people don't spend a lot of time on their hair. Of course, the wind, rain, and snow have opinions about that, as well.

Skin Care

With the wind and other weather factors, you need to make special effort to take care of your skin. Badger Balm and Burt's Bees products are all natural, and available from Swanson Health Products. I use the balm products, not the lotions. Lanolin (a by-product of sheep's wool) is a natural skin protector. I mix it in with balms for additional protection from the wind and cold. (Some people have negative reactions to lanolin, so try a small amount first.)

We also buy NOW Foods grapeseed oil from Swanson Health Products to use as a skin moisturizer. A sixteen ounce bottle is about $8.

Antiperspirant and deodorant products are relatively inexpensive when purchased online. I buy antiperspirant from Amazon.com, where it is actually cheaper than I can buy it in the drugstore in the lower 48.

Shaving Needs

Razor blades and disposable razors can be expensive here in the village, but drugstores in the lower 48 typically have some brand on sale. They are small, lightweight, and easy to ship. If you can find a good deal, stock-up and ship them to yourself.

Swanson Health Products stocks a wide variety of all-natural shave creams. I would stay away from the chemical-filled offerings found at drugstores, unless I was teaching chemistry class. Healthy alternatives are widely available, and competitively priced.

Feminine Needs

Feminine products may or may not be available in your village store, and they may not have the brands that you prefer. Fortunately, both Amazon.com and Swanson Health Products stock a large selection at competitive prices.

Laundry Supplies

The school will probably provide laundry facilities for you. The washer and dryer might be in your teacher housing unit, or they might be at the school. (Undoubtedly, some teachers use the village laundromat.) Either way, you will need laundry detergent. We use Biokleen Laundry Powder, which is very reasonably priced at Amazon.com.

Bathroom, Paper Supplies, and Cleaning Supplies

Toilet paper and paper towels are competitively-priced on Amazon.com, and ship free with your Amazon Prime membership. If the prices seem a little high, put the items on your wish list, or add them to your cart, then remove them. When the price goes down, you'll get an enthusiastic e-mail. I recently bought the 20-roll pack of Scott 1000 bath tissue for $13, which is cheaper than it would be in the lower 48. My 24-roll pack of Sparkle Giant Roll paper towels was about $24 on Amazon. Prices are at least double that in the village store.

You can probably buy your toilet brush, bathroom cleaning brushes, shoe brush, soap dish, dish washing sponges and brushes, and dish towels at Dollar Tree (or any other "dollar" store.) Tie-up the bag from your purchase, and toss it in one of your shipping totes. Remember to buy enough of these items to last an entire year. (They're great for sharing and trading, too!) All of these items are very expensive at my village store. A simple scrubbing brush would cost $7 at the village store.

While you're at Dollar Tree, look for dry cleansing powder (Comet, Ajax, etc.) Also, buy a couple of empty spray bottles if you can find them. The school janitors will probably be happy to fill your bottles with cleaning solutions.

We buy dish soap from Swanson Health Products. They have a large selection all all-natural products at a reasonable price. Seventh Generation is our favorite brand.

Floor Care

You might need to provide a broom and mop for your teacher housing. Ask your principal. If you need them, both the broom and mop can be found, reasonably-priced, on Amazon.com.

Taking Care of the Trash

Your trash disposal protocol will be up to your principal. Most villages have a "dump" where residents take their garbage. (Sorry, street garbage pick-up is highly unlikely.) You may have a central location where you take your trash, and the school maintenance staff will take all of the school garbage to the dump. Or, you may need to take the trash to the dump yourself. You will need some trash bags, unless your school provides them. Amazon.com is a great place to buy kitchen trash bags, with big discounts on large quantities. Consider buying a large supply and splitting the cost with your fellow teachers.

For my trash removal experience, I am responsible for taking my trash to the dump. I pay one of my high school students to take my trash for me. He has an ATV and a cart, and comes around every couple of weeks. He has a very lucrative trash disposal business!

Indoor Plumbing

As I wrote in Chapter 1, many rural Alaska teachers do not have flush toilets in their homes. Needless to say, this presents additional sanitary challenges. However, teachers are able to adjust, with vigilance and cleaning products. I once again remind you to ask about indoor plumbing when interviewing for a job. If you select a village that does not have a waste water system, be prepared for extra effort in maintaining a clean body and home.

Good Hygiene at School

No teacher wants to look out at a classroom filled with boys and girls who are battling sickness. As a teacher, you can emphasize good hygiene at school. Hand sanitizer and tissue should be readily available at all times in your classroom. Regularly wipe down your classroom tables and chairs with sanitizing wipes. Insist that students wash their hands, and cover their mouths when sneezing and coughing. This doesn't mean that you're a "germ-freak." You're certainly not afraid to get your hands dirty. You simply understand the connection between good hygiene and good health, and you want you and your students to be healthy.

Remember, Take Care of Yourself

I hope that in this chapter I have given you good strategies for healthy living in the Alaska bush. Eat good foods, take your vitamins, get plenty of rest, and be ready to take care of minor illnesses. Keep an ample supply of cleaning supplies in your home, and make sure your students are following good hygiene practices in your classroom.

Have a happy, HEALTHY teaching career in rural Alaska!

Uncle Wally's Tip: In Alaska, you'll probably be wearing waterproof shoes most of the time. Make sure to keep them dry inside and out. Athlete's foot can be a real problem. Use foot powder regularly, and keep a tube of Clotrimazole anti-

fungal cream on-hand if athlete's foot symptoms appear. Cracked, itchy feet can be painful. This condition is easily preventable and treatable.

Chapter 5

Getting Around

Travel to the village, from the village, and around the village

If there's one thing all rural Alaska teachers have in common, it is travel. Alaska bush teachers travel great distances to get to their new homes. With the rare exception of the dedicated tribal members who get an education degree and return to their villages to teach, teachers in rural Alaska are from someplace else. Some of us came to Alaska right out of college, while others took more circuitous routes. If you teach in rural Alaska, you have certainly traveled.

Honestly, I've earned a few frequent flyer miles in my day, and I've flown to all four corners of the United States. But there's nothing quite like sitting in the co-pilot seat (as a passenger) watching a bush pilot fly across the tundra, 800 feet off the ground at 120 miles per hour. In the lower 48, I've had automobile commutes of 45 minutes or more on four lane highways and in bumper-to-bumper traffic. But there's nothing quite like riding an

ATV through the village before dawn, with snow falling and the wind gently blowing off the bay.

As I've written several times in this book, we do things a little bit differently out here in the Alaska bush. And there's no better example than the way we travel around our villages, and in-and-out of our villages.

In this chapter, we'll look at both – air travel to and from your village, and ways to get around in the village. The goal here is to give you a preview of what to expect, so that you won't be stressed-out by the unexpected.

Air Travel

By definition, a "bush" community isn't on the road system. You won't be able to drive or take a bus to get here. You will need to fly. (Some people have the romantic notion of arriving by ferry or barge, but the area served by these vessels is small compared to the vastness of the Alaska bush.)

If you're flying from the lower 48, your inbound flight will likely be to Anchorage. More than 15 airlines – large and small – fly over 5 million passengers to and from the Ted Stevens International Airport each year. From experience, the Ted Stevens Anchorage International Airport is a nice, clean, convenient facility. It's easy to navigate and find your way around. People are friendly, and the TSA lines run smoothly and relatively quickly. The airport appears to be well-equipped to handle the winter weather that they face many days each year, and in the many times I've flown through the airport, I've never had a flight delayed or canceled. Overall, I like "Ted-port."

Depending on the size of your village and the schedules, you might be able to fly directly from

Anchorage to your village. Sand Point, Dutch Harbor, and King Salmon are among the many small communities that can be reached by a direct flight from Anchorage. However, most village residents will need to go to a regional hub to catch a flight to their village. Those hubs include Dillingham, Nome, Bethel, Unalakleet, and others.

Without a doubt, your new principal will be able to tell you the best air route to take to your village. My advice: don't get creative. If your principal tells you to go through a certain hub, and take a certain flight, follow their suggested schedule. Benefit from the experience of seasoned bush travelers.

When you book your flight from the lower 48 (say, Denver) understand that your destination city (say, Kwethluk) might not be in the web-site's reservation system. Once again, follow the advice of your new principal on how to book the ticket. You might need to book Denver-to-Anchorage, then Anchorage-to-Bethel on a separate ticket. Then you would need to call the local airline (probably Yute Air) and make a reservation directly for the flight to the village. This can be a bit confusing to the novice, but it works, and teachers fly this way every year.

Arriving in Anchorage

Depending on your time and your budget, you might want to spend a couple of days in Anchorage before heading out to the bush. Anchorage is a great city, and if you've never been there, it's certainly worth a visit. We enjoy the The Alaska Zoo. If you have a rental car, consider driving an hour to the Alyeska Resort, and riding the tram to the top of Mount Alyeska. You can also take your pet for an exam at a walk-in vet clinic, and do some shopping for items to ship to your village. (There's a post office near the airport, and shipping will cost about half the price that it would from the lower 48.) If nothing else, this might be your last chance for a Big Mac or a Double Chocolaty Chip Frappuccino Blended Crème for a while.

Whether you spend two hours or two days in Anchorage, your eventual destination is your new home village. Let's get there!

Flying to the Village

As I wrote earlier, you may be able to take a direct flight from Anchorage to your village. The more likely scenario has you flying to a regional hub first. The airlines that will take you from Anchorage may be unfamiliar to you now, but they will become very familiar to you as you become an Alaskan. Alaska Airlines is a major airline that services most of the regional hubs. They typically fly large jets that transport passengers and cargo to these remote towns.

Ravn Alaska is a smaller carrier that specializes in travel to regional hubs and bush communities. Grant Aviation and PenAir also fly routes to hubs and the bush. These regional airlines typically fly smaller planes, such as the Saab 340 (34 seats) or the Cessna 208 Caravan (9 seats.) These might be the smallest planes you've ever flown on, but these planes and others like them are the workhorses of Alaska aviation. Without these small planes and regional carriers, rural Alaskans would be truly isolated.

The Cessna 208 Caravan serves larger villages.

The Cessna 206 Skywagon serves smaller villages.

You may need to take a different airline (and an even smaller plane) to get to your village. Yute Air provides daily passenger, freight, and mail service to more than 20 bush villages that would otherwise be without air service. You might fly in the Cessna 206, which seats from 3 to 6 passengers, depending on the cargo configuration. This is true bush aviation, and these pilots are skilled, seasoned professionals. It takes a lot of skill to land a single-engine plane on a short, narrow runway in the ever-changing rural Alaska weather.

Buying a Ticket

You're probably very familiar with booking an airline ticket from one major airport to another. However, arranging a flight to a small bush village is a little different.

Typically, buying a ticket on a bush plane to a village requires a phone call to the airline. Your travel agent probably can't arrange the flight, and the airline you need to use might not have an online reservation system. So call the airline, and say, "I'd like to be on the 4:00pm flight to Nightmute on Tuesday." They will ask for your name. When you tell them, they will say, "okay," and that will be it. Don't expect a confirmation number, or a discount for reserving early. Your name is your confirmation, and you pay when you get to the airport. If they didn't have room on the flight, they would have told you at that time. I always call back the day before the flight to confirm.

Your baggage

Make sure to ask the airline that services your village about your luggage allotment. This is especially important if you did some shopping in Anchorage or in the regional hub. If you have too much baggage, you will be charged a freight charge. And don't be surprised if your baggage doesn't make it on the same flight that you take. Several times I have had to return to the village airport to retrieve my baggage on a subsequent flight. Don't stress – it's just part of flying in rural Alaska.

While we're on the topic of baggage, expect someone at the airport to ask your weight. It's all part of making sure the flight is safe, and that's what everybody wants. In fact some airlines will have each passenger stand on the luggage scale at check-in. Like I wrote before, we do things a little differently out here. Aren't you glad I warned you about that?

Regular service

Rest assured that almost all remote Alaska villages are serviced by an airline that has two or more scheduled flights each day. So, if you need to fly to Eek on a Tuesday, you can do that. If you need to get to Kongiganak on a Thursday, you can do that too. Most of these planes also have contracts to carry the mail, as well as limited air cargo. Weather permitting, the planes will fly.

Weather permitting...

Did you catch the impact of that last sentence? Bush planes don't fly in bad weather, and rural Alaska has its share of bad weather. So, it's entirely possible that you won't leave the regional hub airport at the time that you intended. You might leave on the next flight, unless it is booked full. The bush planes fly when the weather permits.

I don't mean to sound discouraging, but almost all experienced Alaska teachers can tell you about a time they got stuck in a regional hub. Sometimes, when the weather is particularly bad, the bush planes are grounded for several days. School district policies vary, but typically if you are "grounded" at a regional hub, your school district will ask you to report to the district office or a local school to work while waiting for the airport to re-open. You might also be invited to sleep on an air mattress in the district office. This multi-day snow-in doesn't happen very often, but if it happens to you, don't be stressed-out. There's absolutely nothing you can do about it, and no one is going to hold you responsible. The weather is no respecter of persons. The next person to get stuck just might be your principal!

Interestingly enough, the airlines typically try to catch-up. If there are five people waiting to fly to Atmautluak, and the 8:15am flight is canceled because of weather, that plane with those people will leave when it can, even if a regularly scheduled flight leaves about the same time. People rarely get "bumped" in bush aviation. When they can fly, then everybody flies.

Also, don't get confused or upset if you see planes flying, and your flight is still on a "weather hold." You see, some planes are IFR (instrument flight rules) and some planes are VFR (visual flight rules.) There are specific meteorological conditions involved, and if you're really interested you can look it up online. But basically speaking, a VFR flight requires a pilot to be able to see where he is, and where he is going. Your bush flight will probably be VFR. The big jets flying from the hub back to Anchorage are probably IFR. Those planes are flown based on cockpit instruments, and can fly in less-than-excellent weather conditions. So, if you're ever stuck in a regional hub, and you see those big jets flying while you're still sitting in the terminal, just remember that your plane is probably VFR, and you're better off waiting for good weather.

The good news is that in late July and early August – the time that you'll be traveling to the village – the weather is usually nice, and flights are rarely canceled.

Charter flights

You may be invited by your principal and/or fellow teachers to join a charter flight to your village. This is usually a good idea, providing you can get to the regional hub by the time the charter is scheduled to depart for the village. Your share of the charter flight will probably cost about the same as your seat on a scheduled flight. The advantage would be that, depending on the number of passengers, you would be able to take extra cargo without paying extra freight costs. Also, you wouldn't have to be concerned about getting a ticket on a scheduled flight in a busy time of the year. Don't be surprised if you're invited to join a charter for your first trip to the village. If you can make it work with your schedule, and the price is comparable, then go for it.

During the flight

If you're riding on a small bush plane, like the Cessna 207 Skywagon, every seat is a window seat. Take pictures. Rural Alaska is amazingly beautiful every season of the year. Surprisingly, I have cell service at several points while flying between the regional hub and my village. You might be able to take a picture with your cell phone and send it to your friends and family in the lower 48. "I'm flying across the tundra. What R U doing today?"

Arriving in your village

The term "airport" has a very different definition in rural Alaska. Out here, the airport is the place where the plane lands. When you disembark your bush plane, the pilot will pull your luggage out of the cargo area, put it on the gravel tarmac and hop back into the pilot seat. From that point on, you're on your own.

Make sure to tell someone from the school exactly when you plan to arrive. Make sure that they understand that you will need someone to meet you and take you to your teacher housing. This is not a problem – in fact, it is expected. However, you have to tell your school personnel of your plans.

Each airline has a village agent in the villages that they serve. The village agent will monitor the VHF radio, and hear the pilot announce that he is just a few minutes away from the village. At that point, the village agent typically drives to the airport to retrieve the mail and cargo on the plane. The village agent will be able to call your principal to let him or her know that your plane will soon be at the airport. Departure times and landing times in bush Alaska aren't quite as exact as they are on big airlines. Some planes have "whistle-stops" on their routes, so your 45-minute flight could take 90 minutes or more. If you tell your principal that you'll be taking the 3:00 PM flight to the village, he will understand that the plane will land sometime that afternoon. It's a good idea to trade cell phone numbers with your principal, just in case.

Of course, you will need to arrange a ride from the airport to the school. Your principal knows this, and will probably dispatch the school maintenance workers to pick you up at the airport and take you to your teacher housing unit.

Leaving your village

It might be the furthest thing from your mind right now, but there will be a time when you need to fly out of your village. When you know the day you want to fly, ask your fellow teachers whom you should contact. In some villages, it will be the village agent. In other villages, you will need to contact the airline directly. Either way, make sure to reserve your seat at least a week in advance. (You will probably pay for your flight at the airline customer service desk when you arrive in your regional hub.)

Because of weather delays, especially around the Christmas holidays (think snow, lots of snow) you don't want to schedule your outbound bush flight too close to your flights to Anchorage or Fairbanks. In fact, many teachers schedule an extra day here and there as a buffer, especially in the winter.

Here's an example: let's say you live in Quinhagak, and you want to fly to Portland, Oregon for Christmas to visit friends and family. Your flight leaves Anchorage Tuesday evening. So, it's a 45-minute flight to Bethel, and an hour flight to Anchorage, so you can leave your village Tuesday morning, right? Wrong! That would be cutting it too close, in my opinion. My advice is to get to Anchorage as soon as you can. Try to leave the village Sunday morning. If you can, great. If not, you have some wiggle room. Let's say that you're able to get to Bethel Sunday afternoon. My advice would be to fly stand-by, and get to Anchorage. Let's say that you get on a flight to Anchorage Sunday evening. Now, you have 48 hours in Anchorage before your flight to Portland. What can you do? My advice would be to get a hotel room. I like the Puffin Inn – it's clean, inexpensive, close to the airport, and near several good restaurants – fast-food and otherwise. After five months in the village, you'll probably enjoy the thought of eating your way through the salad menu at Wendy's.

Okay, maybe you think that's a terrible plan. You'd rather play the odds, hope for good weather, and fly on a tight schedule. That's fine, and it could certainly work. However, my experience tells me to leave a little wiggle room in my flight schedule, especially in winter weather.

When you return to your village, make sure to schedule an extra day or two to accommodate winter delays, and to let everyone know when you plan to arrive. Don't plan to arrive back in your village Sunday evening and teach Monday morning. Flights to the bush rarely work that way.

Transportation In Your Village

Even though you will probably live close to the school, you will need to get around the village at some point. In the rest of this chapter, I'll describe what that looks like.

Cars and trucks

There will probably be a few cars and trucks in your village. In my village, they are more of an oddity than a typical occurrence. I would say we have about a dozen cars/trucks/vans in our village. They are used mostly for work. The school has a minivan used for hauling boxes from the post office, and taking students home on snowy days.

It would be unusual for a teacher to own a car in a bush village. Transporting your vehicle to a village really isn't practical. It would be very expensive and take a long time on a barge. People who own cars in the village typically buy them in Anchorage and have them barged to the village. This adds thousands of dollars to the price of the car. Parts for routine car maintenance aren't available in the village, and must be ordered. Rarely is there a mechanic in the village who knows how to repair a car. And the roads aren't set-up for the typical passenger car. There are probably no street signs or stop signs in your village. Did I mention gas is about $6.50 a gallon?

Walking

Many people get around just fine in the village by walking. It is not unusual to see people of all ages walking on the village roads and boardwalks. It's a way of life, and most village residents are used to it. Students walk to school in all types of weather; most have never been on a school bus.

ATVs

The most common type of motorized transportation in the village is the all-terrain vehicle, or ATV. An ATV is a four-wheeled motorcycle designed for rugged, off-road use. Most ATVs are four-wheel drive, and have racks on the front and  back for hauling parcels and supplies. Teenagers, elders, and every age in between can be seen driving an ATV around the village.

Maybe you've never ridden an ATV, a motorcycle, or anything like that. Don't worry – it will take you about 10 minutes to learn to drive an ATV. Of course, you need to practice so that you can operate the ATV safely. When the roads get icy and the wind starts blowing, you need to be extra-careful. Obviously, this book isn't an ATV manual. Just be ready to encounter this type of transportation when you get to your village.

Depending on the distances that you will need to travel in the village, your desire to explore the areas around your village, and your disposable income, you may decide to buy your own ATV. ATVs aren't cheap. A new ATV can easily cost $7,000. And it will probably cost another $1,000 to get it shipped to your village. ATV dealers in Anchorage, Fairbanks, and Soldotna will be happy to help you over the phone, and will arrange all of the delivery details to your village. All you have to do is send them the money, and wait at the airport. They will also arrange financing. This is a big purchase, and it deserves some careful thought. I just want you to know that the big city ATV dealers are used to doing business this way, and the purchase can be made in a few phone calls.

Typically, everyone in the village buys the same brand of ATV. My advice is for you to buy that brand as well. Our village is a Honda village. About 95% of the ATVs in our village are Hondas. In fact, people here don't say the word ATV. We say Honda. So, it's "Are we taking the Honda to the store?" or "I need some gas for my Honda." If a person has a Yamaha, it's still called a Honda.

Everyone in a village buys the same brand because people in the village know how to maintain and repair them. Also, the village store will stock parts for the popular village ATV. So, if you own a Honda in my village, you can buy your oil filter and your wheel bearings and several other parts at the village store. The guy with the Yamaha has to order all of his ATV parts.

Mrs. Rose and I own a Honda, and I'm glad we bought one. We live about a mile from the school, so it was either buy a Honda, or walk to work. In the snow. Both ways. Also, we get a lot of parcels in the mail from online vendors, and we use the Honda to transport them to our house. (Remember, in the village you probably won't have mail delivery to your house.) Additionally, our Honda is our entertainment. We ride somewhere almost every day after work. Sometimes we go to the hills, and sometimes we ride down to the beach. In the fall we go up the mountain to pick berries. The Honda makes all these trips possible.

An option to buying an ATV by yourself would be to enter a partnership or co-op with other teachers. I can see two or three teachers who live close together easily sharing an ATV. Of course, there would always be scheduling tasks. But the money savings would be substantial. Something to consider, certainly.

There are typically one or two used ATVs in the village for sale at any given time. To that, I would offer a heartfelt caveat emptor – let the buyer beware. I personally did not consider buying a used ATV in the village.

About half of the teachers in our school own an ATV. The other half borrow the school's Honda, or rely on fellow teachers or the school custodians to fetch parcels and provide occasional rides. The choice will be yours to make in the near future. When you get to your village, you will quickly see if an ATV purchase makes sense for you.

Snow machines

To begin with, people in Alaska don't say "snowmobile." We say "snow machine" or "snow-go." Whatever you call it, you're probably familiar with these machines – skis on the front, and tracks on the back. In some northern bush villages, snow machines are prevalent, and used for daily transportation. In other villages, they are more for recreation. Once again, you will discover how snow machines are used in the village when you arrive. I would say that when compared to ATVs, fewer teachers own snow machines.

Boats

Some teachers and administrators in the Alaska bush own boats. As you would imagine, they are used mostly for fishing activities.

Transportation to-and-from the village and around the village is certainly an important part of your rural Alaska teaching experience. Plan your air travel carefully, remembering the differences in major-airline flights and bush flights. And when you get to your destination, evaluate your need for transportation in and around the village.

Uncle Wally's Tip: When you're flying, pack a sandwich, some nuts, and some fruit. The journey from your home in the lower 48 to your village will probably take at least a couple of days. When you're hungry, being able to grab a snack out of your carry-on is a real treat. And let's face it – airplane food is not what it used to be! On flights to Alaska and within Alaska, it's certainly not uncommon to see your fellow passenger reach in his pocket and pull out a peanut butter-on-Pilot-Bread sandwich!

Chapter 6

Keeping in Touch

Communication in rural Alaska

After reading the previous chapter about transportation, you might feel a little bit apprehensive about how far away from friends and loved ones you might be traveling. That's natural, of course, because...well...*it is a long way!* But the distances can be reduced or eliminated with good communication with your friends and family back home. In this chapter, we'll look at the availability of modern communication in rural Alaska.

Before we get to the details, here are a few important points. First, different villages may have different communication opportunities. It's certainly not within the scope of this book to research the Internet speeds of every village in the bush. That's something you can easily determine for yourself, especially when you have your job search narrowed down to two or three villages. Secondly, realize that communication developments are subject to change. A few years ago there was no cell phone service at all in bush Alaska. Now, most (if not all) villages have cell phone service. Once again, a few questions to your principal will keep you informed about your communication options.

One more thing: stay in touch. Remain in contact with your friends and family in the lower 48. The distance and remoteness of bush Alaska makes it easy to forget the outside world. Sure, you'll make new friends in your village; some of them you may eventually consider "family." Communication with your contacts back home is quick, easy, and relatively inexpensive. Don't lose touch with your emotional support network. These are the people who know you best. But remind them of the time difference! You probably can do without "good morning" texts at 3:00am!

Phone Service

Do all Alaska villages have phone service? That's impossible to say. As soon as I claim that fact in writing, someone will find a village with no phone service. Let me just say that it is likely that all villages that you consider for employment will have some type of telephone service. Of course, those services include landline and cell phone service.

Landline

With the emergence of cell phone technology, fewer people are seeing the need to install and maintain a landline. This has been true in the lower 48 for several years. As cell phone service is becoming commonplace in rural Alaska, landline use is down here as well. Mrs. Rose and I don't have a landline here in the village. In fact, our principal is the only school professional who has a landline in our village. (Of course, the school has a landline system, but it's based on the school computer network.) People in the village are often out-and-about fishing, gathering, visiting friends, shopping, getting the mail. Cell phones are the natural choice for village life.

If you decide that you would like to have a landline, your principal can help you contact the phone company. Chances are, only one company will offer service in your village. It is not prohibitively expensive, but probably more than you're used to paying in the lower 48.

Cell phone service

Cell phone service has been a recent step forward in rural Alaska communications, and most village families have at least one cell phone. It is very typical for high school students, and even junior high school students to have their own cell phones, just like in the lower 48. (Some Alaskans receive cell phone assistance through the Lifeline program.)

For the first few years, GCI was the only company to provide cell phone service to rural Alaska. Recently, other companies such as TelAlaska Cellular and Alaska Communications have begun to offer service as well. At the time of this writing, competition hasn't reduced prices. However, we are hoping that prices will go lower soon with the influx of new cell phone carriers. Cell phone service is probably a bit more expensive than you're currently paying. Mrs. Rose and I are GCI customers. We share 1200 minutes a month (two phones) and have unlimited text. We pay $76/month plus tax. If we had unlimited minutes, it would be about twice that amount. That's a nationwide plan, meaning that we can use our phones when we travel to the lower 48 without additional roaming charges. We own our cell phones, so we're not under contract.

The pay-as-you-go, no-contract, unlimited-everything cell phone plans that are gaining popularity in the lower 48 aren't available out here. We're waiting, and hopeful.

Okay, that's talk and text. What about data plans? Currently, rural Alaska cell phone service doesn't support data. We have 2G service, which is talk, text, picture messaging, and some very basic data functions. As of this writing, 3G and 4G haven't made it to the Alaska bush. The companies tell us that it's coming, but we're not holding our breath. So, right now, you won't be able to stand on the tundra and access your favorite smartphone apps.

Our cell phones from the lower 48 are useless in Alaska. We had to buy new phones when we got cell phone service here. The cell phone companies sell phones, just like in the lower 48, and if you sign a two-year contract, you can get a pretty good deal. Smartphones are actually pretty common out here. People use them as talk-and-text cell phones, as well as portable Internet devices on a Wi-Fi network. So, if you really have to have a Smartphone, it's doable, but you might need to buy a new one when you get to Alaska, and you will be able to access your apps only when connected to Wi-Fi. Of course, you should verify that for yourself before making any purchases. Cell phone services, plans, and requirements can change very quickly.

Uncle Wally's Tip: You want to use iPhone or Android apps, but you don't want to shell-out hundreds of dollars for an Alaska-compatible smartphone. Here's the solution: buy a simple talk-and-text cell phone, and also a refurbished device that can access Wi-Fi, such as an iPod Touch or a Kindle

Fire. That's what I did, and saved hundreds of dollars. I found a refurbished iPod Touch online for less than $100, and it runs all of my apps on my home network, and the Wi-Fi at school. I can even Skype on the iPod Touch. Yes, it's a little bit cumbersome being a "two-device" guy, but you quickly get used to it.

Internet Service

Once again, I have to be careful to say "most"...but high-speed Internet access is available in most moderately-sized Alaska bush communities. Some communities have dial-up speed, which works for e-mail, and not a whole lot else. And like cell phone service, it's a bit more expensive, and a bit more limited.

Internet service plans

Our Internet service provider is GCI. Our plan costs $75 per month, but we get a $15/month discount because we have our cell phones with GCI also. Our speeds are pretty peppy. But here's something we had to get used to: this is not unlimited Internet access. Our plan gives us 15 gigabytes per month. For an additional $40, we could get another 10 gigabytes per month. This is enough Internet to get us through the month using e-mail, browsing web-pages, ordering online, using tablet apps, downloading eBooks, etc. It is not enough to stream movies or Internet radio, or download large media files, such as movies or large music collections. If we go over our limit, we are charged one cent per megabyte. If you do the math, you'll see that this can get real expensive real fast. We can log-on to the Internet provider's web-site to determine how much Internet we have used, and how much we have left in the billing period. I check this every day.

Of course, this chapter is all about staying in-touch with friends and family. Although 10 or 15 gigs a month isn't enough Internet to support a Netflix account, it is certainly enough to send e-mail and upload images. The people back home will want to hear from you, and see pictures from Alaska. Your limited Internet access will let you meet these goals.

Uncle Wally's Tip: Instead of attaching pictures to each e-mail that you send friends and relatives, upload your image files to a free online cloud service, like DropBox or Microsoft Onedrive. You can send links to the pictures that you store  in the cloud, or give your friends and family the username and password to the cloud account. This will save your Internet usage, and everyone still gets to see your pictures.

It's reasonably easy to check the Internet availability in villages that you are considering. Ask the school district or principal which company/companies offer Internet service to your village. You can call the companies directly, or check the rates online.

Starting Internet service

If you're living in teacher housing, chances are Internet access has already been installed there. If that's the case, starting home Internet service might be as simple as making a phone call to the provider and attaching your wireless router to the connection. Installing Internet service to a house that's never had it before is a little bit more involved in the bush, but not tremendously complicated. Our high speed Internet comes to our house wirelessly from a tower in the middle of our village. I had to buy an antenna/receiver from GCI, and mount it on the side of my teacher housing unit. The antenna/receiver is about the size of a quart milk carton, and came with the Internet cable to connect it to the house. (It is possible to mount the antenna/receiver inside the house, but we were told we'd get better reception by mounting it outside.) One of my friends who had recently mounted his antenna/receiver mounted mine for me in a few minutes. After a phone call to GCI to register the device, I was online, and we haven't had any problems with it at all.

Once again, realize that not all remote areas have high-speed Internet. Some places are still using dial-up speed service, which is probably coming over residential phone lines. I would imagine the communications companies are working to provide high-speed Internet service to these villages as well, but it's probably not a cost-effective venture for the company. In the meantime, we just have to be patient and hope for the best.

High-speed Internet at school

If high-speed Internet is available in your village, your school will probably have the fastest service in town. Many village schools rely heavily on videoconferencing technology to provide quality instruction to high school students when the course content goes beyond the training and certification of the generalist teacher at the site. This technology requires unlimited, high-speed Internet during the school day.

Principals typically have no problem at all with teachers coming to school after school hours to use the Internet. If you're really fortunate, your teacher housing will be close enough to the school to connect to the school's wireless Internet hubs. This arrangement will save you money, and provide excellent Internet service to your teacher housing. While free Internet in your housing probably isn't enough reason to select a village, it does represent a nice benefit. School-provided Internet could save you several hundred dollars per year.

Videoconferencing with Friends and Family

If you have unlimited Internet service at school or in your teacher housing unit, you can take advantage of free videoconferencing via Skype. You are probably already familiar with Skype. In fact, you may have used Skype for your interviews for your Alaska teaching job. If not, the Skype web-site can do a better job of describing it than I can. Basically, you and your friends and family members download the Skype software onto your computers. Everyone is assigned a Skype username, and you can add each other to your contact list. Skype "calls" are placed over the Internet, and video can be added from your web-cam once the conversation begins.

As of this writing, there is no charge for this part of the Skype service. Skype also has a paid option that allows you to call landlines and mobile phones from your computer, either on a per-minute basis, or a month-to-month basis. Also, there is a paid membership level that allows videoconferencing between three or more computers. (Currently, only one conference participant needs to have this advanced membership for the group videoconferencing to work.) As with all video services, Skype is subject to change in pricing and service, and may be have changed since this book was written in 2014. Still, it's worth a look as another inexpensive (or free) way to keep in touch with family members.

If everybody is running Mac OS, then FaceTime is certainly a viable option. Most Mac users are familiar with this built-in videoconference app on iMacs, iPods, and iPhones.

Mobile apps for Skype are available for Mac OS, Android, Windows Phone, and Kindle Fire HD systems. As of this writing, FaceTime is available only for Mac devices. That's not likely to change, as FaceTime is a very popular Mac feature, and Apple features FaceTime heavily in advertising for iPhone and iPod Touch. Whichever system you choose, make sure that your desired contacts are on-board before you move to Alaska. If you're making a check-list of things to do before moving to rural Alaska, write down "practice videoconferencing."

Of course, if you have a limit on the amount of Internet data you can use, videoconferencing probably isn't a viable option for your teacher housing. There are many variables to consider when estimating the amount of data that a Skype or FaceTime videoconference uses. Checking the user forums results in a wide range of mathematical equations. But I think it's safe to say that videoconferencing will sap your allotted data allowance very quickly. The alternative is to use videoconferencing at school, with your principal's permission, of course. Realize that teacher retention is a big issue out here, and principals understand that keeping in touch with friends and family back home is important to teachers. In other words, they want to keep you here, and if you're happy, you'll be more likely to stay. Tell your principal your videoconferencing plans first, but it's a fairly common practice out here.

Social Media and Blogs

Many teachers keep-up with their friends and families in the lower 48 using social media services (Facebook) or perhaps by starting their own blogs. Both are free, simple, and highly-effective.

However, I need to warn you to be very, very, VERY cautious about your use of these services when you enter your professional life. Comments on blogs or Facebook pages can easily be misinterpreted. In a small town – in or out of Alaska – almost everyone is the parent, grandparent, aunt, uncle, or cousin of a student at your school. A comment or posting that would be a minor ripple in a big city can become a tidal wave in a small community.

Here's a scenario. (It is based on an actual occurrence, but the details have been changed.) A new teacher is invited to a feast in the village prepared by the tribal community members. She samples a wide variety of foods, and describes some of the more unique foods - such as akutaq, muktuk, and seal oil – in casual, less-than-flattering ways in her online blog. The next afternoon, she is called into her principal's office and informed that community members have become offended by her descriptions of their traditional foods. She immediately apologizes to her hosts, and posts a sincere apology on her blog. Unfortunately, the cloud hangs over her head for the remainder of the year, and she transfers to a new school the next year.

The teacher in the fictional example above meant no harm. She was describing her experiences for her friends back home, who probably knew her to be a somewhat picky eater. They would be proud that she is trying new foods, even if she finds them distasteful. But this is the Internet. She did not consider that local residents could read her blog, and wasn't aware that this was the case.

Here's another fictional example. A new teacher is invited to go fishing with two village tribal members. This, of course, is an honor, as it represents not only acceptance, but an acknowledgment that this new teacher is deserving of a portion of the community resources. Everyone has a good day of fishing, and the biggest fish of the day escapes the line of one of his tribal member companions. That night, he posts some photos on Facebook, and writes that his companion "choked, and let the biggest fish get away, LOL!" In a culture where subsistence living is vitally important, a person typically shouldn't joke about someone else's misfortune in subsistence activities. Although the unfortunate person may laugh about it himself, joining-in typically isn't appropriate. When confronted with the Facebook posting, the new teacher immediately apologized both in-person and online. However, the social damage was done, and he certainly wasn't invited on any more fishing trips.

Did the new teacher mean any harm? Of course not. He was simply doing what he and his fishing buddies back home do all the time – tease each other about "the one that got away." However, this communication was misinterpreted, with disastrous results.

I hope that the two fictional examples above drive home the point that in a culture that is new to us, our comments can easily be misinterpreted. In a small community, such missteps can have long-lasting, far-reaching effects.

Now, at this point, some of you might be thinking, "Wait a minute, those two teachers were just joking around. They didn't mean anything." I totally get that thought. I'm sure that the teacher tasting seal oil for the first time made quite a facial expression. (I know I did!) And I'm sure that her hosts had a good laugh, just as the fishermen laughed about the big fish that escaped the line. These personal experiences became problems when they were posted online for the whole community, and the whole world to see. That's where it crossed the line, unintentionally or not.

I'm sorry if you expected this section to recommend starting a blog about your Alaska teaching experiences, or posting your reactions to village life on your Facebook page. I'm not going to make that recommendation. I want you to always have positive relationships with the people of your village, and there's really too much at stake.

My personal advice (and that's what this book is, right?) would be to give up the Facebook page while in Alaska, unless you can be absolutely, positively sure that your comments can't be taken the wrong way. Blogging is even more public than a Facebook page, and should also be approached with extreme caution. If you decide to continue posting or blogging, then my advice would be to write about yourself, and your personal experiences. Focus on the things you are learning, and approach the culture with a great deal of respect. For the first few weeks, ask a teacher who has lived in the village for a while to read your posts before you post them. You have worked hard to achieve your position as a rural Alaska teacher. Don't jeopardize it with a misguided online post.

So – how can you use the Internet to keep your friends and family informed? How can you share your personal feelings and reactions with your loved ones? Is there any place that you can share your fears and frustrations, without having your emotions visible to everyone? Yes. My advice is to set-up an e-mail list, and invite your friends and family to join. Most free e-mail services offer this, and it's pretty easy to set-up. Every weekend you can write an "Alaska Update," include links to pictures in your DropBox account, and send it to exactly whom you want. Of course, you still want to have class and personal integrity as you write about your experiences, but you can "let your hair down" with people who already know you, trust you, and won't be offended if you're having a particularly bad day.

Mail

As you keep in touch with your loved ones in the lower 48, don't forget those who don't use the Internet. Some of your senior friends and family members may not have a computer, and may never have one. People in this group depend on and greatly value cards, letters, and pictures. I know, you could send an e-mail and say, "Please share this with Grandma," but it's just not the same.

Here's something you probably haven't thought about: you likely won't be able to buy a greeting card in the village. My advice is to buy a box or two of note cards (blank inside) and bring them with you to Alaska. You can use these cards for birthdays, anniversaries, or just "thinking-of-you" times. Mailing costs are the same across the United States, so a card or letter will mail for less than fifty cents. That's a bargain! And my experience is that people are thrilled to receive a piece of mail "all the way from Alaska!"

Of course, realize that mail sometimes doesn't travel as quickly as we're used to in the lower 48. Bush mail depends on bush planes, and bush planes don't fly in bad weather. Sometimes our mail is stalled at the post office for several days until the weather clears and the bush planes fly again. Expect about 10 days for a letter mailed from bush Alaska to reach the east coast. Priority Mail will get there in about 5 or 6 days. That's assuming clear weather and regular mail flights.

What about sending digital images to people who don't have e-mail? Once again, that's an easy fix. Set-up an online account with Walgreens, upload your Alaska pictures, and have your order shipped to your family members in the lower 48. As I write this, Walgreens will print a 4" x 6" picture for 20 cents, and ship it for another 12 cents. So, you can send a dozen photographs to your grandparents for less than four dollars. I know that now most people send e-mails instead of cards, attach pictures rather than putting a photo in an envelope, and even read books online (like this one.) But there's still a certain part of the population that loves to hold a greeting card and a photograph. Make sure that you don't leave those people out of the loop when you move to Alaska.

Finally, while we're on the subject of mailing items, you might want to include a small object, such as few pebbles, a bird feather, or a little sprig of tundra grass when you mail a card or letter. I have found that this is a real treat for people in the lower 48, most of whom will never visit the Alaska bush. Try it, and see how your friends and family respond to "a genuine piece of Alaska!" (Tip: snow doesn't ship well!)

Television

Okay, so television isn't technically a way to communicate with your loved ones, but some people want to know about TV reception out here, and this is a decent place to include a paragraph. In simple terms, most of rural Alaska has access to hundreds of TV channels through DISH Network and DIRECTV.

The pricing is comparable to what you'd pay in the lower 48. However, obtaining and installing the equipment will probably be different. In the lower 48, the satellite TV technician will come to your house, mount the satellite dish on your roof, run the cable through your attic, and attach it to the tuning console and your TV. This will probably cost you nothing, or a very small installation charge.

In rural Alaska, you will need to order the dish and tuner, and probably pay for it as well. Then it will be up to you to get it installed. You probably won't be the first person in town to sign-up for satellite TV service. In fact, my experience is that a large number of village households have satellite TV service, and there's probably someone in the village who can help you set it up. Also, the dish and equipment may already be installed in your teacher housing, courtesy of the district or the previous teachers. So, obtaining satellite TV service may be as complicated as ordering and installing equipment, or as simple as making a phone call. You can ask your principal or future fellow-teachers about TV, if it's important to you.

Or, it might not be important to you at all. Mrs. Rose and I don't have a TV. We have found plenty of things to keep us busy in Alaska. We get our news from the Internet. We read, write, take photographs, explore our hobbies, and generally experience rural Alaska. As odd as it might sound, you might want to think about giving-up TV when you move up here, or at least trying to go without it for a few weeks. Television can become an obligation, as you strive to keep up with your favorite shows. There are lots of opportunities for recreation right in front of me in rural Alaska. I can watch TV any time. Right now, I want to live the Alaska life.

Moving to Alaska will probably be the biggest move any member of your family has ever made. You will be a legendary part of your family history! Just make sure to keep in touch with friends and family. Fortunately, with the appropriate technology and a little planning, you can remain in contact with your loved ones while living your Alaska adventure.

Chapter 7

Managing Your Money

Financial services when the nearest bank is 100 miles away

I admit it. Before I moved to rural Alaska, I was old-school about money. I got my monthly paycheck at school and stopped by the bank on the way home. I liked going into the bank lobby. Maybe it's because my mom used to take me to the bank when I was a kid, and that was pretty special. The bank lobby had a fountain-type orange juice dispenser, and I'd get a paper-cup full of orange juice. Then I would join my mom at the teller window, and the teller would hand me a Dum-Dum lollipop. After the bank visit, I would get my 25-cent weekly allowance. Life was good at the bank.

When I lived in the lower 48 I would sit at the dining room table and pay my bills by check every Saturday morning. I never used an ATM. I never accessed my accounts online. I used a debit card for local purchases, but that was just about my only foray into 21st century banking.

Now that I live in rural Alaska almost all of my banking is done online. You've probably taken care of your finances that way ever since you opened your first checking account. But if not, get ready to make the switch!

In this chapter, I will describe to you the way that I manage my finances when the nearest bank is more than 100 miles away.

Your Banking

You will definitely need a bank account when you move to rural Alaska. Even if your move to Alaska is several weeks away, you should begin this process well in advance. Some people advise setting-up your new bank account when you get to Anchorage or even your regional hub. This doesn't make sense to me. My trip to Anchorage, prior to moving to the bush for the first time, was a very busy time, and filled with many other tasks. I'm glad that I already had my Alaska finances in order before getting on the northbound plane.

Based on my research, the two banks with the most branches in Alaska are Wells Fargo and First National Bank Alaska. Keybank would come in a respectable third place. Do you have any of these banks in your current city or town? If so, it makes sense to open your account, in-person, at your local branch.

That's how I chose Wells Fargo. Both Wells Fargo and First National Bank Alaska have branches in my regional hub. And Wells Fargo also has a branch in my hometown in the lower 48. So, Wells Fargo was a natural choice for me. When I was sure I was moving to Alaska, I withdrew a small amount of money from my existing bank, and opened a Wells Fargo account. Over the next few weeks, I built-up the balance of my Wells Fargo account, while allowing my existing bank account to gradually deplete. Of course, I kept careful track of my existing bank account, as I was still using it as my main account. By the time we left for our trip to Alaska, most of my money was already in my new Wells Fargo account. I made sure that my existing bank knew about my move, and made arrangements to close that account from my new Alaska home. That was a bit sad, because I had been a customer of that bank for many years. However, they don't have any banks in Alaska, and it just makes more sense to go with a bank that does business in your state.

At this point, you might be saying, "That's nice, but I'm still in college, and I have exactly $72.46 in my bank account." So, your transition to an Alaska bank won't be quite as cumbersome as mine. However, I would still advise you to have an account with an Alaska bank as soon as possible. Get established, get the debit card, and that's one less thing you have to think about.

While you're at your new bank, ask them for direct deposit information. You will need this when you report to your school site. Most banks can print a form that has all of the information the school district will need to directly deposit your paychecks. As far as I know, all school districts offer direct deposit, and some districts require it. This is really the only paycheck option that makes sense in rural Alaska.

When you open your bank account, you will probably be offered the opportunity to order some checks. My advice would be to wait until you arrive in your village and you are assigned a post office box. You will want your new Alaska address on your checks, and until you get settled, you probably won't know the address. Before leaving the bank, make sure you have all of the information for ordering your checks by mail. You probably won't need many checks. I write one or two checks a month, if that.

Of course, you want to pay special attention when your new bank explains about online banking. At home, online banking is probably just a quick way to check your balance. Here in rural Alaska, it's our main method of banking. I complete almost all of my banking tasks online, including checking my balances, paying bills, transferring money from checking to savings, and sending money to other Wells Fargo customers. Wells Fargo will even print checks and mail them for me, to pay people like the dentist and to send donations to local charities who don't have elaborate online banking services.

The only banking task that is a little bit odd is depositing a check I receive in the mail. For example, earlier this year I attended a meeting at my school district office, and I got snowed-in. The airport was closed, and I couldn't get home. So, the school district took me to a nice bed and breakfast, and covered my meal and taxi expenses until I could leave the next afternoon. The next month they mailed me a check to cover those expenses. Very nice! Okay – I live in a remote Alaska village. What exactly am I supposed to do with a check? The answer: mail it to the bank. I called the branch in my regional hub, and they gave me the address and the instructions. (First they referred me to their app and instructed me to take a picture of the check. I tried three times, and it didn't work like it does on TV.) So, I put the check in an envelope, put a stamp on it, and mailed it the next day. Within a few days, the amount was deposited into my bank account.

Cash

If you've searched the Alaska teacher blogs and forums, you've probably found many opinions about the need for cash in a village. Some people claim that they never need cash in the village, so they don't make a point to keep any. Other people come to the village with lots of cash and use it for all of their purchases. I find that a moderate approach works best. I bring some cash with me to the village, because sometimes, you just need cash.

How much cash do you need?

I can't tell you how much cash to bring to the village. I can tell you things for which I use cash. I use cash to buy an occasional school breakfast and lunch. I use cash to mail cards and letters at the post office. I use cash to make occasional small purchases at the village store. That's about it.

So, if you plan on buying your breakfast and lunch at school, mailing a lot of letters, and buying a candy bar on the way home from work, you might need $40 or $50 per week. That would be on the extreme high end, in my opinion. Your school cafeteria might take a check, and that would decrease the above figures significantly.

Really, there's nothing else in the village for which I need to pay cash. The village store – really the only place to buy anything – accepts my debit card with no problem. You might buy a little fish or a little caribou meat here or there from a village resident. If that's your desire, budget a few dollars in cash for those purchases as well.

I bring about $500 in cash to the village when I arrive each semester. I usually leave the village with most of it. But I'm glad I have it. When we fly out of the village, and arrive in a regional hub and eventually Anchorage, it's nice to have some cash in my wallet for snacks, vending machines, and other small purchases.

Where can I get cash?

Most villages have no branch banks and no ATMs. You can search for ATMs on your bank's web-site, but be aware that short distances are irrelevant when there are no roads out of your village. If you have a good, community-oriented store, they will probably cash a check for you. I know that our store provides this service at no charge.

In some ways, it feels a little bit like summer camp – you have a certain amount of money, and it needs to get you through a certain amount of time. Sometimes teachers have the opportunity to travel to a regional hub for school district meetings, and they often stop by the bank to get some cash for themselves and/or their fellow teachers. Really, your opportunities to get cash are quite limited.

Credit Cards

If you've read the previous chapters, you know that Mrs. Rose and I buy most of our food and clothing online. Of course, you can use your bank debit card for these transactions, but you can also use a credit card.

Selecting a credit card

Here are some ideas for selecting a credit card. Most airlines have a Visa or American Express credit card that earns miles for their frequent flyer plan. If you buy your groceries, clothes, housewares, and airlines tickets with this credit card, you can eventually accumulate enough miles for a free ticket. Many airlines offer a substantial number of miles for simply accepting their card.

Also, look for a credit card that has some sort of buyer protection plan, especially as it relates to the warranty, and to shipping. If you want to make a major household purchase – perhaps a large television or a new computer – you will want to use a credit card that offers these guarantees. Shipping to the bush can be rough on electronics, and sometimes purchases get "lost" in transit. You want a credit card company that will protect your purchase, and work on your behalf if your expensive item is never delivered.

Here's a sad story that I heard from a fellow teacher: he saw a television on sale in the regional hub newspaper, and called the store. After confirming the price, he mailed the store a check for the TV and freight charges. He waited... and waited... and waited. The television never arrived. The store verified that they had made the shipment. It was too late to stop the check. The television simply disappeared. Unfortunately, the teacher was left with no recourse, and it was another year before he saved enough money to purchase another TV. Of course, this time he used a credit card!

Uncle Wally's Tip: Of course, everybody knows this, but I'll say it anyway – you really want to pay-off your credit card bill every month. Carrying a balance can increase the amount you pay for goods exponentially over time. As a teacher, you will certainly have enough income to buy food and clothing. It's those other purchases that can make a credit card hard to pay-off.

Making credit card purchases for other people

Some teachers also use their credit cards and debit cards to make online purchases for village residents, especially people who work at the school. From my personal observation, very few village residents have bank accounts and credit cards. It just isn't part of the economy in many villages. If they want to order something from a catalog, they have it shipped C.O.D. If you're not familiar with that, C.O.D. stands for Cash on Delivery or Collect on Delivery. Customers place an order C.O.D. and pay for it when it arrives at the post office. Before Internet shopping and widespread credit card use, a great deal of catalog shopping was done C.O.D. This is still pretty popular in the villages, but the number of companies that accept C.O.D. is dwindling.

I'm telling you about this because you might be confronted with this situation, and you want to think about it before you're faced with it. Someone in the village may ask you to place an online credit card order for them. They will give you the cash, and of course you pay the credit card bill when it comes in. I have been asked to do this by people who work at my school, and I have absolutely no problem with it. They do great work at our school. They have taught me a great deal about living in the village, and if they want to order something from an online vendor, I'm happy to help. They typically have the cash in their pocket, and they are paying me before I get the confirmation e-mail.

But what if the requestor was a village resident whom I didn't know, or what if they were ordering something of which I didn't really approve? In that case, I believe I would decline. And please understand, that type of request has never happened. But it could happen, and I know how I would respond because I have thought about it. My hope is that now you have thought about it, too.

Like most things in rural Alaska, managing your finances takes a little bit more planning, and is accomplished a little bit differently. I'm glad my remote circumstances pushed me into a modern banking experience. But, when I'm back in the lower 48, I hope it's okay if I stop by the bank for orange juice and a Dum-Dum.

Chapter 8

Bringing Your Stuff

Transporting your personal belongings to rural Alaska

Most of us have moved at least once in our lives. Some people have moved once or twice, and others have moved more frequently. I have moved a few times myself, and the method is typically the same: start scouting the stores for good moving boxes; slowly pack away items you won't need for the next few weeks; start loading boxes into your car, and then delivering them to a new location. Sometimes I borrowed a friend's van or rented a U-Haul. Maybe you've been involved in some longer, more involved moves that used professional movers and big semi-trucks. I've never done that myself, but it must be pretty popular, because I've seen many of those trucks on the highway.

As you can probably imagine, teachers traveling to the Alaska bush don't have the luxury of loading-up a van and driving to the village. Like most everything else around here, moving your personal belongings is accomplished by airplane. As you have probably predicted after reading the previous chapters, moving is just a little bit different up here, and takes some extra time and careful planning. But it can be done! In this chapter, I will offer my tips for moving your personal belongings to Alaska.

Analyzing Your Move

Your cross-continent move is a big deal, so it's worth a little bit of thought before beginning. Here are two important questions to ask before you begin.

Question #1: What will you *need*?

This is a question for your principal, and if you're really fortunate, you can also ask the person who is currently living in your future teacher housing unit. You need to have a good understanding of what is currently in the house/apartment, and what will not be there when you arrive. Believe me; this varies greatly from district to district, and village to village.

Having this information can save you a lot of headaches, and money as well. Let me give you a personal example. When we moved into our first teacher housing unit – a stand-alone house in the village – we were surprised to find that there were no curtains on the windows! Fortunately, Mrs. Rose is ingenious and creative, and fashioned some make-shift curtains from sheets and blankets. Remember that in August the days are very long, and it doesn't get completely dark until around 11:00 PM. So the curtains were important for darkness, as well as privacy. I think it was our second day in the village that we ordered some "blackout" curtains from an online vendor. It took about three weeks for those to get here, and I think we paid more than we would have at Walmart or K-mart in the lower 48.

Here's another example: do you rely on a microwave oven? Your teacher housing unit may not be equipped with a microwave. Amazon has a great selection of reasonably-priced microwaves. Of course, there's no reason to buy one if there's already one in your teacher housing.

You get the idea. This is one of those situations where you can't be afraid to ask questions. Realize that your future principal may not know the answer to these questions. Your best resource is the person who is currently living in the teacher housing unit.

Before leaving this section, let me tell you about a practice among teachers in Alaska that I have heard of, but not experienced. Sometimes teachers leaving the village will offer to sell household items to the future teacher, and leave the items in the teacher housing unit. If you get friendly with that teacher, you may want to bring-up the subject. Once again, use your best judgment, and if it works out for both of you, then great.

Question #2: What will *you* need?

Wait a minute... same question as the first one, right? Not exactly. In answering this question, think about what you personally need to feel comfortable in a new place. Maybe you're a "camper," who is comfortable living with what you can cram into a duffle bag and a couple of cardboard boxes. Maybe you're a "nester," who doesn't feel at home unless you're surrounded by family photos and knick-knacks. Perhaps you love to cook, and you can't imagine living without your cookware, knife set, and small appliances. Rest assured, no one's going to tell you what you need to leave behind. But it is important to examine what you'll really need when you move to Alaska, rather than just the things you are accustomed to. Your life will be different in many ways when you move out here. Some of the things you thought you couldn't live without may just stay boxed-up in your teacher housing closet.

Moving Supplies

As you know, there are no roads connecting bush communities with the rest of Alaska. Fortunately, there's an organized system that moves millions of items every day: the United States Postal System. Yes, the same postal system that you use in your current location is in full operation here in the Alaska bush. I call it the "Uncle Sam Moving Company." I am happy to report that when Mrs. Rose and I first moved our clothes and household belongings to Alaska, we had 100% success rate. In this section, I will share our shipping methods with you.

Before I continue, I need to thank everyone who shared their experiences on blogs and online forums. Like any good researcher, I took a little here, and a little there, added my own parts, and came-up with this method.

Totes

A tote is a large plastic bin used for storage. It is also your main moving box to bush Alaska. All totes are not created equal. Some totes are designed strictly for household use, and other totes can handle tough scenarios – like a move to Alaska. Don't skimp on your totes. The cheaper ones can warp, crack and break. The totes that you need probably won't be available at a  discount store (Walmart, etc.) Home Depot and Lowes both have outstanding heavy-duty totes. I have used totes from both stores. They are both excellent, and very similar. As of this writing (2014) the Home Depot tote is the "HDX 27-gallon Tote." The Lowes tote is the "Commander 27-gallon Tote." Both totes are black with a yellow lid. Depending on where you live, you can expect to pay $10-15 per tote. (Of course, that information can change.) Both stores put totes on sale occasionally, so if you have a few weeks to plan your move, you can shop the sales.

Whether or not you choose to use these exact totes, here are some features to look for:

- thick, sturdy sides and bottoms. The tote should not be easily bent or pushed-in. The material will not crack when pushed or bent.

- rectangular design. Don't go with an overly-rounded or bulbous tote. Wheeled totes are useless.

- 27 gallon is a good size. This allows you to pack the tote while staying under the weight limit. Larger, full-packed totes will be overweight, resulting in extra charges and possible delivery delays.

- securely stackable. Your totes should stack on top of each other when full, and inside each other when empty.

- separate lids. Hinged lids can break off.

- pre-drilled holes in lids, with corresponding holes in the top of the tote.

Uncle Wally's Tip: At this point, some readers are probably thinking about using cardboard boxes instead. Certainly, this can work, although I would not advise it.

In rural Alaska the mail gets delivered, but it can be tough on boxes and parcels. Sometimes (not often, but sometimes) cardboard boxes from vendors arrive smashed-in, with crushed corners, half-open, and a little bit damp. When you're thinking about shipping your clothes, your housewares, and your personal belongings, a sturdy tote is your best bet.

Cable Ties (zip-ties)

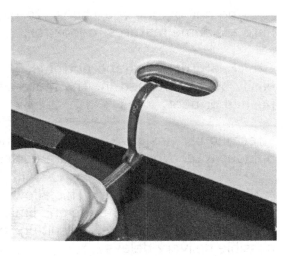

A cable tie (also known as a zip-tie) is a strip of plastic designed to secure electrical cables, such as those used in TV and stereo systems. We will use our cable ties to secure the lids to our totes, via the pre-drilled holes. You want to buy the heavy-duty ties, not the cute little ones. I buy cable ties from Amazon, in a pack of 100. They have a tensile strength of 120 pounds, and are about 11 inches long. You will need three to six cable ties for each tote. (There are six holes, but three or four will probably be enough to secure the lid. Your choice.)

Strapping Tape

Strapping tape is high-quality packing tape, reinforced with fiberglass strands. I use the Duck Brand strapping tape, about 2 inches wide, with a tensile strength of 300 pounds.

Clear Packing Tape

I use the Scotch heavy duty shipping tape.

Additional Items (that you probably have around the house)

Paper, a black permanent marker (Sharpie.) I also use clear sheet protectors (one for each tote) which you can buy at the office supply store.

Optional items

Some people use the "Space Bags" that connect to the vacuum cleaner to decrease the size of their packed clothing. This might work for you, although I've never used them to ship things to Alaska. Realize that the bags make items smaller, but the weight is about the same.

A postal scale might come in handy. I bought a digital postal scale from Amazon for about $25. It gave me a good idea of how much to pack in each tote, and about how much the postage charge would be. You can check the postal service web-site to estimate rates.

Standard Post

Please consult the United States Postal Service web-site (usps.com) for information about shipping. You will be using Standard Post to ship your totes to Alaska. As the web-site reads now, the maximum weight for a tote is 70 pounds, but my totes were typically around 40 pounds. Once again, I strongly encourage you to visit the post office web-site for information on Standard Post before you begin packing your totes.

Here's something that I did before my "moving trip" to Alaska. I took one of my empty totes to my local post office, and I asked to speak to the postmaster. I told him that Mrs. Rose and I were moving to Alaska, and showed him the totes we planned to use. He was actually interested in my plans, and by the time my last tote had shipped, I felt like the workers at the postal counter were part of the team! The postmaster approved my tote, gave me suggestions about securing the lids, and showed me where I could stack my totes while I waited in line. Overall, it was a professional experience, and I am glad I took the time to meet with the local postmaster.

Our shipping time from the southeastern United States to the Alaska village was about three weeks using Standard Post. We made a point to have all of our totes shipped right after July 4th, and everything was accounted for and waiting for us when we arrived in the village near the first of August. (Thanks again to the school maintenance workers who accepted the shipments and had all of our totes, as well as our Amazon orders, waiting for us in our teacher housing unit when we arrived.)

Media Mail

Media mail is much less expensive (and a bit slower) than Standard Post. You can save money by grouping your media mail items together, and shipping the entire tote or box media mail. According to the USPS, "*The material sent must be educational media. It can't contain advertising, video games, computer drives, or digital drives of any kind.*"

Your New Address

As soon as you accept a position with a school district, ask your new principal for the address of the school, and where you should ship your personal belongings. This is unusual, and even awkward, by lower 48 standards. But, your principal will be expecting for you to ask, and will already have an answer formulated. Typically, he/she will give you the school's address, which will probably be a P.O. Box number.

The principal and teachers will probably leave over the summer. But the school maintenance workers, who are likely full-time village residents, will be in the village during the summer when your totes arrive at the school. The school probably has a procedure for new teacher parcels. Perhaps the maintenance workers stack the boxes and totes in the gymnasium. As I shared earlier in this book, I was very fortunate as the school maintenance men delivered my totes and boxes directly to our teacher housing unit.

Realize that your village post office will likely be relatively small, and they won't be able to store your totes until you arrive in August. I addressed my totes so that the village postmaster would have no doubts as to where they belonged. The address I used was:

New Teacher Wally Rose
Name of the School
P.O. Box number of the school
Village name, AK Zip code.

For the return address, I used a family member's address. I used the computer to make full-page mailing "labels" printed on plain printer paper. I printed several copies.

Packing Your Items

You probably understand the concept of packing clothing items in an orderly way to maximize the space. One additional suggestion would be to use clean plastic grocery bags to group smaller clothing items, such as socks, underwear, and T-shirts. That way, when you open your totes you can pull out your bag of socks, your bag of underwear, etc.

You can use your towels and blankets as packing material for your fragile items. Also, use your towels to fill the empty spaces in your totes to prevent the smaller items from jostling around during transit. To avoid your items shifting around, you should pack your totes snugly, but do not over-fill. You want the tote lid to fit without snapping off, and you don't want the sides of the tote distending.

Here's my procedure for packing:

1) Before closing the lid of your tote, toss in one of your full-page address sheets. Also, make note of the contents of the tote, and keep a running log on an electronic device or in a notebook. My notebook entries include the number of the tote, the general contents, the approximate weight, and the date that I mailed it.

2) Place the lid on the tote. The pre-drilled holes on the lid and on the lip of the tote should match. On the totes that I used, there are six holes, three on each long side. Insert a cable tie in each set of holes, and tighten the lid in place. Don't over-tighten the cable ties. We need a little flexibility so they won't snap if forced. Use a short strip of packing tape to tape down the ends of the cable ties. This will keep the postal workers from getting

scratched. Do not clip the ends off of the cable ties. That would make the ends even sharper!

3) Use two strips of strapping tape to secure the lid from long-side to long-side. Make sure to run the tape into the crevices and down the sides an adequate length.

4) Use two additional strips of strapping tape to secure the lid on the ends.

5) On one of your full-page address sheets, write the words Standard Post. Also, number your tote for your reference. Place this address sheet in a plastic sheet protector.

6) Using the clear packing tape, securely attach the page protector containing your address to the tote lid.

7) On a smaller piece of paper, write your name and new Alaska address and tape this to the side of the tote. Completely cover the small address label with clear tape. This is your back-up address label, if something happens to the large address label on the lid.

Congratulations! Your tote is now ready to ship.

At the Post Office

My advice is to take your totes to the post office two or three at a time. That way, you're not overburdening the postal staff. The postal counter employee who serves you will be responsible for weighing your totes and moving them to the back room. There's a big difference between two totes and five totes.

Depending on the "friendliness" of your post office, you may be offered a dolly to help you move your totes from your car to the counter. There is probably a place that you can put your totes near the counter while you wait in line, so that you don't have to continuously scoot them along the floor as the line moves.

Remember to ask for Standard Post. It was probably their duty, but the postal workers always ran-down my delivery options... "Next Day... Priority..." and I would chuckle politely. It would cost a fortune, but I would like to see them try to deliver a tote from the southeastern United States to my Alaska village in one day! Each tote typically cost about $40 - $50 to ship, depending on weight. My personal opinion: that's a bargain. I certainly wouldn't or couldn't deliver it for less.

Tracking Your Shipments

Standard Post comes with a tracking number. After a couple of days you can enter that number at USPS.com, and track your tote. (Tip: type all of your tracking numbers into a word processing document, separated by commas, and you can copy-paste your tracking numbers into the USPS.com web-site all at once.)

Be aware that the level of tracking service for Standard Post is a bit less specific than Express Mail or Priority Mail. From my experience, Standard Post tracking will give you a record that the package was received, perhaps a few stops in between, and when the package is "Out for Delivery." When I shipped my totes, I got city-by-city updates on some of the totes. Other totes appeared to be stuck in one nearby location for several days, only to indicate "Out for Delivery" the next day. My advice is to keep track of your totes, but don't depend on Standard Post's tracking for daily updates. All of our totes arrived in the village within a few days of each other.

Items to Consider

In this section, I want to mention some items that you will want to consider bringing or ordering, based on your personal needs and tastes. Some of these items may already be in your teacher housing unit, so ask if you're able to.

For the Kitchen

- at least one pot for cooking and heating food

- a frying pan

- a pan or glass dish for baking

- a set of knives

- wooden spoons; spatula, tongs, can opener

- storage containers for leftovers

- silverware, dishes, bowls, mugs, drinking glasses

- a measuring cup

- a dish draining rack

- a crock pot for cooking soup and stew

- a popcorn popper (if you don't use microwave popcorn)

- a microwave oven

- a coffee pot

- a quart metal Thermos for coffee and tea

- a tea kettle; useful for heating water, even if you don't drink tea

- a colander for washing and draining fruit and vegetables

- dish towels, sponges, dish scrubbers

- Ziploc bags (sandwich, quart, and gallon), freezer bags, and trash bags.

For the Bathroom

- bath towels

- toilet brush

- plunger

- soap dishes for sink and shower

- towel rack

- shower curtain and rings

- toilet paper holder

- toothbrush holder

For the Bedroom

- sheets, blankets, comforters

- pillows

- small electric heater fan

- alarm clock

General

- brushes for cleaning, especially shoes

- power strips and extension cords

- flashlights

- curtains

- waste baskets

- rechargeable batteries/battery charger

- bungee cords, rubber bands, twine, paper clips

- a folding one or two-step stepladder

- a wireless Internet router

- laundry detergent

- light bulbs

- family photos and colorful decorations as desired

- binoculars

- a small household tool kit

- scissors

- a hair cutting device

Bring This, Not That

Here are more packing tips.

Bring this: Kindle, Nook, or other e-reader

Not that: Stacks of books

Books are heavy and cumbersome. As much as I love books, in Alaska I read on my Kindle.

Bring this: iPod or other MP3 player with docking station or speakers

Not that: Stereo system

You may have the best stereo system in the state, but it's probably not wise to try to ship it to the Alaska bush. A nice pair of headphones provides a great musical experience.

Bring this: Your laptop computer

Not that: Your big-screen TV

Packaging and shipping a big screen TV from the lower 48 would be a monumental, expensive task. I'd say you'd have a 50-50 chance of getting it here in one piece. If you need a big TV (and you probably won't) then you can buy one online when you get here. That way, the vendor will be responsible for getting it to the village safely, and shipping might even be free.

Bring this: Your laptop computer

Not that: Your desktop computer

You might have the latest tricked-out computer with a huge monitor, but shipping it to the bush is a perilous proposition. Most bush schools rely heavily on computer technology, so they should have what you need. And you may not have room for a desktop set-up, especially if you have a roommate. Bring a nice laptop instead.

Bring this: Rugged clothes, and one nice outfit

Not that: A varied, balanced wardrobe

It is good to have one nice outfit – khaki pants, white dress shirt, tie, blue blazer – to wear in the village on very special occasions. But the other 90% of your wardrobe should probably be "rugged" style – jeans, cotton shirts, sweatshirts, fleece jackets. A nice wool sweater can dress-up any outfit. Of course, check with your principal. But my guess is that jeans will be the standard attire in your village school.

Bring this: Colorful items for decorations

Not that: Dark, earth-tone items

You will see plenty of beautiful greens, browns, and blues out here. But some of the brighter, more vibrant colors are rarely seen. Of course, all of this is a matter of personal taste. Just make sure to select household decorations that truly brighten your teacher housing unit.

Using a Storage Unit

Unlike the moves described at the beginning of this chapter, your move to rural Alaska probably won't involve taking everything you own. It is important to be selective when every item you bring must be mailed and the charge is determined by the weight. The smart move is to arrange storage space with a friend, a family member, or a local business. Friends or family members may be happy to "support" your Alaska adventure by allowing you to store some items in their garage, basement, or attic. You can also find storage businesses that rent a wide variety of storage units – from closet-sized to garage-sized – in most medium to large communities. When you return to the lower 48 after the first year in the bush, you'll have a good idea of what you need to take back, what you should continue to store, and what you'll probably never need. Each trip back gives you another opportunity to reassess your storage needs.

A "Shipping Buddy" in the Lower 48

It is a true blessing to have a "shipping buddy" in the lower 48 who can mail boxes to you if you need them. If you are truly organized – and I hope you are – you can box similar items together for storage. For example, you might have a box marked "extra long-sleeved shirts." If you need those shirts, you can have your "shipping buddy" tape-up the box, put a shipping label on it, and mail it to you in Alaska. The alternative, of course, would be to either buy more clothes online, or just do without. This is also true for household items that you might need. It is wonderful to have a friend or family member who will pick-up needed items at the store and mail them to you in Alaska. It may be uncomfortable to ask someone to do this for you. Ask yourself, "Would you do it for them?" If so, they will probably be happy to help you as well. You can always return the favor when they need help.

Moving clothes and household items is an important task for the new rural Alaska teacher. Fortunately, the supplies for shipping are easily available, and the United State Postal Service will ship parcels to any address with a zip code. If you use the proper containers, carefully select and ship only what you need, and plan ahead, your personal belongings should be waiting for you when you arrive in your new village.

Chapter 9

Rural Alaska Life

We've covered quite a bit so far in this book. I've given my advice on food, clothing, shelter, health, and packing. Of course, there are always more things to tell you. In this chapter, I'll cover some of the additional topics you might be wondering about. These topics weren't quite complex enough to merit their own chapters, but I think you'll find the information useful. That's my hope, as always.

What's a Village Really Like?

Wow. That's a tough question, but it's a question that's probably swimming around in your mind. Exactly what is a village like? Of course, there are dozens of villages in rural Alaska. I've been to a few, and met several teachers from other villages. I'm sure that each village has its own unique characteristics. Let me try to make some general statements in the following paragraphs. Remember, there are exceptions to every situation.

Land, tundra, water, and boardwalks

Most villages have at least three of these, and some have all four. Your rural Alaska village will probably be on the water – either a river, a bay, or the sea. This reflects the village's reliance on fish and marine mammals as an important part of their subsistence activities. The water also provides transportation among the villages, which was especially important before the bush planes flew regular routes.

The tundra

Also, your village will probably have a certain amount of tundra. The tundra is a treeless area covered with thick moss, grass and lichens. During the winter, the tundra can be frozen solid. In the late spring, summer, and early fall the tundra can be very, very soggy. Walking through soggy tundra can be nearly impossible. The thick mosses cover wet mud. You will probably find yourself ankle-deep in mud if you try to walk too far on the tundra. Once I was in a teacher meeting, and we were all asked what we had learned so far this year. One new teacher said, "The tundra is not a shortcut!" That's a very important rule to remember. You won't see native Alaskans walking across the wet tundra. Therefore, you probably shouldn't blaze the trail. Not all tundra areas are impassable. In the summertime, berries can be harvested from many tundra areas that are firm enough to walk on.

These wild berries were gathered on the tundra.

You might have been amused to find "land" in the heading for this section. Don't all villages have land? Yes, but some villages have much more solid ground than others. Houses typically can't be built on the squishiest sections of tundra, as the foundations (or stilts) would sink deeper into the ground. Some villages have a system of boardwalks instead of gravel roads. The boardwalks are shared by pedestrians, ATVs, and bicycles.

Gravel roads

I have not seen an asphalt-paved road in a bush village. They may be out there, but I haven't seen them. The roads are hard-packed earth, covered with gravel. Most villages have a road department with tractors that spread gravel over the roads when needed. Depending on the village, gravel is either barged-in, or obtained from a local mountain. If your village is the source of the gravel, then your road department will have more gravel to work with.

Airport

Your village will almost certainly have an airport. Just remember, in rural Alaska the word "airport" means "the airstrip where the plane lands." Don't expect passenger-accessible buildings, ticket counters, waiting areas, or snack bars at the airport. When it is time to catch a flight, you check the schedule, go to the airstrip and wait.

Alaska village airports typically have well-maintained gravel runways. After a snowfall, village workers are usually busy on their tractors, maintaining the runway so the planes can land.

The Post Office

Remember, in rural Alaska there is no door-to-door mail delivery or pick-up. Everyone goes to the post office to get their mail, and to mail letters and parcels. Of course, the mail is very important to us out here, and we receive a lot of our supplies from online vendors and mail-order companies. From my experience, just about everyone goes to the post office at least two or three times a week. I go every day. It's between the school and my teacher housing unit, so it makes sense to stop on the way home. When you're new in the village, the post office is a great place to meet people. People will ask, "Are you the new teacher?"

Every residence in town has a post office box at the post office. There are a few large P.O. boxes, but most of them are small. Still, you should be able to receive most of your letters, magazines, and catalogs in your P.O. box. If you have a large envelope or a parcel that won't fit in your box, the postmaster will put a notice in your box, and you can pick up your parcel at the counter.

A village post office provides the services that you would find in any post office in the lower 48. You can buy stamps, ship parcels, and access services such as Priority Mail and Express Mail. This is America; this is a post office.

In medium-sized and larger villages, the post office is open during regular work hours; something like 9 AM to 5 PM. If the post office has only one employee (which is typical,) it may be closed at lunchtime. In smaller villages, the post office may be open at only certain times of the day. Of course, you will want to become familiar with your village post office's hours of operation just as soon as you get to the village.

The Village Store

Second only to the post office as a place to "see and be seen" is the village store. In Chapter 2 I wrote about what food is typically available in a village store. If you have an excellent village store (like ours) you can buy a variety of food (canned, boxed, and fresh) as well as socks, hats, simple hardware items, motor oil, and a small selection of toiletries and over-the-counter medicine. If you live in a larger village, your store might be a member of the AC (Alaska Consolidated) chain.

Unfortunately, some village stores are below average. They may be operated with only profit in mind, meaning that they stock only items that sell quickly, such as candy, chips, and soda. Other stores may be operated out of someone's house, and open for just an hour or two a day. I mention this because the quality of the village store really impacts the quality of life in your village. As I wrote earlier, we have a very good village store that is open 6 days a week, and stocks a nice variety of items. Sure, the prices are higher than you'd pay in the lower 48, but they are really in line with prices in our regional hub, and probably better than prices in other villages. In fact, when people from outside the village visit, they often make a point of shopping in our village store and taking their purchases back home.

Uncle Wally's Tip: Realize that there is an unwritten etiquette to follow when paying for your purchases at the village store. There probably won't be a standard check-out line, like you're used to in the lower 48. Instead, customers will stand in  a half-circle around the cash register with their items. When the cashier finishes with a customer, the remaining customers look around the half-circle, and it is decided who goes next. Typically, village elders are always next. Mothers with small children are often served early in the process. Customers who have struck-up conversations with other customers typically wave-off their turns. The first time you shop in your village store, watch and learn. Don't be surprised if you're skipped over a time or two. But if the cashier says, "Oh, it's our new teacher. Come on up here," then accept the offer and place your basket on the counter.

Community Buildings

Expect to see some buildings built and maintained for the benefit of the community. These buildings will include the health clinic, city hall, a tribal affairs office, a laundry facility, a church, and perhaps a community center. If your village is a member of a fishing cooperative, then they will probably have a facility in the village as well.

Law Enforcement

Someone in the village will be responsible for law enforcement, however this will probably be different than you're used to in the lower 48. Most villages have a Village Public Safety Officer (VPSO) who is trained as a first responder and is authorized to conduct basic law enforcement activities. The VPSO will probably have an office in or near the city hall, and it may even include a cell to temporarily detain offenders. In a small-to-medium-sized village, the VPSO probably won't be a full-time officer. However, he/she will always be on-call to handle emergencies. The VPSO typically appears at the school in uniform once or twice a month. He/she can be a great resource for your classroom, and may ask to speak to your class about a safety, curfew, or mischief issue.

The Alaska State Troopers are stationed at the regional hubs, and they will be dispatched to a village as the need arises. Typically, they travel to the village at the request of the VPSO, or to investigate a crime report or complaint received at the Alaska State Trooper office. In many cases, the offender will already be in the custody of the VPSO when the trooper arrives. In other cases, the trooper will conduct an investigation, just like any other investigating police officer. Typically the trooper will stop by the school and visit with the teachers and school administration, just to keep in touch. Like the VPSO, an Alaska State Trooper is usually a great guest speaker.

The tribal office may employ one or more law enforcement officers as well (perhaps on a part-time basis.) These officers have authority to enforce local ordinances, such as curfew and property issues. They also serve as first responders, and are especially responsible for the safety of the children and the elders in the village. Tribal officers will also appear at the school at times, especially if they want to reinforce a safety concern, such as the need to be careful on the ice.

ATVs

As I wrote in Chapter 5, the All-Terrain Vehicle (ATV) is the major method of transportation in the village. ATVs are driven by everyone from teenagers to elders. It is very common to see five or more ATVs parked outside the village store and the post office.

Almost no one in the village has a driver's license, and typically all ATV riders observe standard motoring courtesy. However, there are no lines painted on the road, and probably few road signs (or none at all.) Our village has one STOP sign and two speed limit signs. I think there is one traffic light in our entire school district. Of course, you do want to exercise care if you are a pedestrian.

Not a 9-to-5 atmosphere

A village typically doesn't run on a 9-to-5 workday, like the town or city that you're used to. Before I moved to Alaska, I joined the rush-hour traffic twice a day. A steady stream of vehicles entered my medium-sized city in the morning, and returned to the suburbs in the afternoon. It's definitely not that way in the village. Most village residents don't punch the time clock. Subsistence activities are typically scheduled by the dictates of the activity, not the clock. The school's time-constrained schedule is the exception in the village, not the rule. In the winter months the village may receive only four or five hours of daylight each day, and the village activities during that time will decrease. Conversely, in the summer when the sun sets at around midnight, village residents may work very long days fishing, hunting, gathering, and preparing for the winter months.

Housing

From my experience, houses in the village are typically closer together than the typical suburb in the lower 48. (Of course, many people in the lower 48 live in apartments and townhouses.) Typically speaking, you don't see the landscaped "yard" in a village. The land surrounding the house is typically used for storage, and fish-drying. Land is typically filled with tall tundra grass, which is never mowed. In the winter, the grass dies back, and forms an underlying layer for the snow. The deep roots of the tall grass prevent the soil from washing away when the snow melts in the spring.

Storage trailers

Many houses in the village have a separate storage trailer outside the house. These trailers have various informal names in different villages. Typically, the storage containers are rectangular, about 12 feet long, 5 feet wide, and 6 feet tall. Some are wired for electricity. Food, tools, and household goods are stored in these trailers. Some people store their snow machines in their trailers when they are not in use. Some trailers contain workbenches, and serve as workshops.

Lifelong residents and relatives

In most cities in the lower 48, very few people are lifelong residents. However, in your village it will be very common to meet many people who have lived in the village their entire lives. In many cases three or more generations will live in the same house – grandparents, parents, and children. Visiting relatives always have a place to stay. Also, you will find that many village residents are related to many other residents, either by blood or by marriage. I remember during my first year of village teaching, I drew a circle on the board, and wrote a student's name in the circle. I asked that student to name all of the other students she was related to, and I tried to draw a graphic organizer on the board. After a couple of minutes I ran out of space! Extended families are prevalent in rural Alaska villages.

Community feasts

You will probably experience several community feasts during your first year in the village. Feasts are part of many village gatherings, such as weddings, funerals, and holidays. The school gymnasium – often the largest room in the village – is often the natural choice for the feast location. You will have the chance to attend these feasts, and it's a great opportunity to serve the community members. I typically keep a pot of coffee brewing in the school kitchen during the feast. After the meal as the people are circulating, I walk around and serve coffee. It gives me a chance to meet many new people in a humble role. Most people smile, nod, and say "Quyana," (thank you.)

The Weather

I guess any book about Alaska would be incomplete without some mention of the weather. Whenever I talk to friends and family in the lower 48, they invariably ask about the weather. Most people associate Alaska with COLD, and yes it does get cold up here!

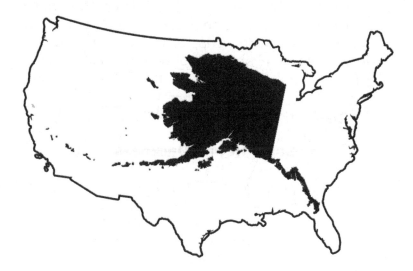

But realize that Alaska is a huge state, and the weather in Sitka is very different from the weather in Barrow. In fact, Sitka in southeast Alaska is about 1,200 miles from the north slope town of Barrow. That's about as far apart as Miami and New York City. So trying to make general statements about the weather in Alaska is a lot like making general statements about the weather on the east coast of the USA.

That said, the Internet is a great place to find historical weather data. You can easily find the expected temperature for your village for any month of the year. Precipitation records are also available, but less reliable.

Smaller villages may not report rainfall, resulting in lots of zeroes in the historical weather databases.

Cold is certainly an accurate word to describe most of Alaska most of the time. But realize that like everywhere else, Alaska's weather is determined by high and low pressure areas, storm fronts, and weather systems. Prevailing winds can bring warm air from the south, or frigid air from the arctic. One week, we'll be talking about how unseasonably warm it is, and the next week colder weather will move in and we're wearing our snow boots and fur hats.

And yes, it does get cold here. Very cold. Cold.

Sunlight and Darkness

One natural phenomenon that is easy to track is the amount of daylight that your village will get each day. I downloaded an app called "Rise" onto my iPod Touch. With the "Rise" app you can type-in the name or zip code of the villages you are considering, select a date, and see just how much daylight you can expect. A few degrees of latitude can make a big difference. If your village is above the Arctic Circle, there will be days when the sun never rises above the horizon (although there will be a bit of twilight on most days.) In the northern hemisphere, the winter solstice is the shortest day of the year, so you might want to research that date first. (The winter solstice will be either December 21st or 22nd)

Of course, most places in Alaska have at least a little bit of sunshine every day. In my village on our shortest day, first daylight appeared around 8:45am and the sun rose at about 10:45am. That same day, the sun set around 4:50pm, and it was totally dark at 6:30pm. So, we had about six hours of sunlight on our shortest day.

Yes, it was strange looking out the window during third period and seeing darkness. And I had to hustle after school to get to the post office and home before dark. But, once your shortest day is reached, every day is a little bit longer. In fact, we add about four or five minutes of sunlight each day. As I write this in mid-February, we're up to 9 hours of daylight, with about 90 minutes of twilight in the morning and the evening.

Undoubtedly, some of your friends and family members will say, "I could never live in Alaska, without seeing the sun all winter." The myth of "months of darkness" is one you'll have to dispel for your friends in the lower 48.

Your Family in Alaska

When I taught school in the lower 48, it seems like just about every teacher was married, or got married soon after they began their teaching careers. I don't have any statistics to back this up, but it seems like most new rural Alaska teachers are single. They move to the bush as individuals, and basically don't need to be concerned with maintaining a household. But some new Alaska teachers will move to the bush with a spouse and perhaps children in tow, ready to make a new life on the last frontier.

Your Spouse

My sincere advice is that if you move to rural Alaska with a spouse, make sure that they are in total agreement with the move. You really don't want to undertake a totally different lifestyle with someone who is, at best, lukewarm to the idea. If you've read the previous chapters, you understand the challenges you will face. A spouse can provide support, unconditional love, and humor as you confront these challenges. However, if one of you is unhappy from the start, the challenges will be amplified.

Reading this book with your spouse, and having discussions about your move to the bush can certainly help you cement your priorities and expectations. I am reminded of a story that I read about a newlywed teaching couple who moved to a rural Alaska village. They hadn't done a lot of research, and first learned when they entered their teacher housing that they didn't have a flush toilet. The man was fine with it, but the woman was instantly in tears. The lack of indoor plumbing was a point of contention, and the couple didn't return for a second school year. Talk about what's important to you, and make the final decision as a couple. Spend many hours in earnest conversation with your spouse, and make sure that moving to rural Alaska is really what they want, too.

If your spouse is a teacher, then you will almost certainly be working at the same school. (Most villages have one school that serves all grade levels.) You will both be entering rural Alaska with well-paying jobs, and a built-in support system. However, if your spouse is not a teacher, their prospects for employment in the village will be severely limited. Most villages have very few wage-based jobs, and those jobs traditionally are held by tribal members. The "classified" jobs at your school – maintenance, secretary, classroom assistant, cafeteria worker – are among the few jobs available in most villages, and are typically held by tribal members. So basically, your spouse shouldn't expect to go to the village and "find a job."

Of course, there are certainly opportunities to keep an industrious spouse busy. There will likely be someone in the village willing to teach the newcomer about subsistence activities. A spouse who provides food for the family is certainly "working." Many teachers' spouses are raising children in the home, which is a full-time job. A spouse may be able to make a few dollars providing child care service for other teachers. Some spouses take up handicrafts, become accomplished cooks, take online classes, or write that novel they've had swimming-around in their heads for years. An industrious spouse may relish in the opportunity to get away from the activities and responsibilities of suburbia, so that they can pursue previously-ignored interests.

Your Children

If your children are school-aged, then they will certainly be welcomed in the village school. Many village schools are dealing with decreased enrollments, and teachers' children will earn more funding for the school. Recently, I read about a rural Alaska school that was actively seeking a teacher with three or more school-aged children. In Alaska, schools with fewer than ten children are funded at lower levels, and this school was projecting only seven students. Perform an Internet search for "Alaska small school closings" and you will find news articles about this phenomenon.

You need to evaluate the school as a good fit for your children, just as any parent would do. Many rural Alaska schools operate under a dual-language model at the elementary level. Elementary students are taught at least part of the day (and sometimes all day) in the native language of the area. This is the language that most students hear at home. Of course, your first-grade child would probably have no experience with the native language. If you are a parent, the educational needs of your child certainly should factor in to your decision to teach in bush Alaska.

That said, many teachers raise thriving families in rural Alaska. Their children are certainly gaining experiences that their peers in the lower 48 can only dream about. Some of these families have a spouse who home-schools the children. Other teachers' children are fully integrated into the village school system. Make sure to ask questions, and select your village with the total welfare of your family in mind.

Religious Opportunities in the Village

Almost all villages have at least one Christian church. The denominations may be different from those you are used to. Two denominations found frequently in rural Alaska are the Russian Orthodox Church and the Moravian Church. Catholic, Baptist, and Assembly of God churches are among the other denominations found in rural Alaska. You can certainly find more about these denominations on the Internet.

The impact of religious life certainly varies from village to village, so it would be fruitless to make even the most general comments here. Realize that a small village will likely have one church, and larger villages will have two or more. Some smaller villages do not have full-time clergy. Visiting clergy and lay-pastors often minister to the congregation.

Realize also that an Alaska bush church service may be conducted totally or in-part in a language other than English. That language may be a native language, or it may be a language closely associated with the denomination.

I have been to rural Alaska church services where the entire service was conducted in the native language. In another village church I visited, a line was read in the native language, and then the same line was read in English.

What Should You Do With Yourself?

When I lived in the lower 48, life kept me busy. It seems like I always had a list of things to do and places to go. Those plans could include grocery shopping, getting the oil changed in the cars, stopping by the dollar store for a few items, going out to eat, picking-up the dry cleaning, mowing the yard, buying some new socks. These things kept me busy.

When I moved to rural Alaska, most of those tasks disappeared completely. I was able to undertake other tasks, like shopping and bill-paying, much more efficiently using the Internet. I found myself with a lot of free time, and quite frankly, I didn't know what to do with myself.

Before moving to the bush, Mrs. Rose and I decided that we would try to live without television. Really, we weren't very big TV-watchers anyway, and I never liked paying for hundreds of channels that we never watched. We've stuck to that decision, and I'm very glad we did. I probably would have spent a lot of that free time watching television, which is generally not productive time for me. We brought a big box of DVDs to watch, but we haven't watched one in several months. We have found things that we like better than watching television.

I started writing books again. I say "again" because I wrote several nationally-published teacher resource books before I moved to Alaska. The book you are reading is actually the second book I have written this school year. I enjoy writing. It is very relaxing for me. The whole Amazon/Create Space self-publishing system has opened the door for me to write books about topics that appeal to smaller audiences. I don't have to be concerned about finding a publisher or making a lot of money. I'm writing about things I enjoy, and I hope that I'm helping people along the way. I have ideas for three other books to write after this one is finished.

Mrs. Rose has always been a very good cook, but she has increased her skill and creativity in the kitchen since moving to Alaska. She is also developing her skill in knitting, crocheting, and weaving. She is creating new designs for hats and headbands, and enjoys creating handmade items for her friends. She has also taken-up photography, and she has a great collection of pictures. Recently she learned how to use photo-editing software, and worked to digitally restore some old family photos that we scanned-in last summer.

You might decide to use your free time in a totally different endeavor. If you are a new teacher, you will probably spend a certain amount of time "creating" your classroom and developing your teaching materials. You might also need to read ahead in the textbooks and become more familiar with the scope and sequence of the classes you are teaching.

How about taking a few online classes, or starting work on your Master's degree? There are certainly plenty of opportunities for online education. Maybe you've always wanted to learn another language or study graphic design, but you never had the time. There are online classes on these topics, and hundreds more.

Of course, there are many other hobbies out there, including painting, carving, cooking, and needlework. Maybe you could learn to make web-pages, become certified in office software applications, or learn about all the ways to use that SmartBoard hanging in your classroom.

Maybe you've never really studied the Bible, and it's been a while since you've considered the role that God plays in your life. You can probably join a Bible study group in your village.

Of course, you're now living in the biggest state in the nation, and there's a lot to learn right outside your door. Everyone in the village will know that you are the "new teacher," so don't be afraid to show people that you are interested in learning about the things that make your village special. You probably want to stop short of inviting yourself, but if you let it be known that you want to learn how to prepare dried fish, or set a net for trout, or make salmonberry jam, you'll probably be invited at some point.

Maybe you'll join me in leaving the TV and the video game system behind when you move to rural Alaska. Use your time to explore your surroundings, learn the culture, and develop your interests. Alaska is an exciting, often challenging place to live. You can live your life, or you can watch TV, but it's hard to do both.

Any time you move to a new place, there's a lot to learn. Certainly, rural Alaska presents a learning curve that is a little steeper than most. Enter your village without preconceived notions about how things "should" be, and instead ask yourself why certain things work on the tundra in ways that they really wouldn't in the lower 48. Remember that "different" isn't necessarily "bad." Realize that the pace of life will be slower in the bush, not because there's nothing to do, but because your life won't be filled with appointments, shopping trips, and obligations. Be prepared to use your newly-found free time wisely, and make the most of your Alaska experience.

Chapter 10

Your Pets in Alaska

Man's Best Friend on the Last Frontier

If you're not a pet owner, this chapter may have very little interest to you. But if you consider yourself a "dog-person" or a "cat-person," you probably can't imagine making the trip to Alaska without the company of your faithful companion. In this chapter, we'll look at the considerations for pet ownership and travel in rural Alaska.

Bringing Your Pet to Alaska

In most cases you will be able to bring your pet to Alaska. Teacher-owned dogs are fairly common here, and several teachers also bring cats from the lower 48. Of course, you would need to ask your principal about that during the interview process.

(Honestly, I have no idea about other types of pets, such as fish, birds, reptiles, and small mammals. That would be something to ask your principal or school district about.)

I think the common thought among school administrators is that pets are important to many teachers' happiness, and a happy teacher returns to the district for a second and third year. A new teacher who misses his/her dog or cat back in the lower 48 is less likely to return.

Mrs. Rose and I own a fluffy 10-pound dog who gets along just fine out here. He has an easy-going personality, and wakes-up excited to greet the world every day. He keeps us entertained and is a good companion. Here are some things that we've learned along the way to help you with successful pet ownership in the Alaska bush.

Don't Buy a New Pet Now

Don't buy a dog or cat specifically to bring to bush Alaska. There are too many variables in the equation. Will you have a roommate? If so, your roommate (who perhaps has been living there for several years) might already have a pet. Our small dog is friendly, but I can't imagine him sharing an apartment with a house cat. Of course, pets of the same species are sometimes incompatible as well. Or perhaps your new roommate is allergic to cats. These are all things that you need to consider before bringing a pet to your village.

Your district may have a no-pet policy for teacher housing. Additionally, it's probably not a great idea to bring a new puppy or kitten into a furnished housing unit. You'll be spending your days in your classroom; do you plan to crate the dog all day? And I wouldn't want to have to explain to my new principal that my puppy chewed-up the new couch in my teacher housing unit.

There will probably be opportunities to "adopt" a pet in your village if you decide that you would like to be a pet owner. In a village, this is an informal process. In our village, we have several dogs that roam, and there always seem to be a few puppies trotting around. Determining true ownership of the pups might be a daunting task, but typically if you talk to the owner and offer a few dollars, you will find yourself the proud owner of an Alaskan bush dog! Purebred and AKC registered? Not a chance. But you will have a dog genetically pre-disposed to thrive in the Alaskan winter.

I have seen one cat since I arrived in this village. It belongs to one of our teachers. I have never seen a cat walking around the village. Maybe some villages have cats, but ours doesn't.

Uncle Wally's Tip: The Pribilof Islands – St. Paul and St. George – are located about 700 miles west of Anchorage. They don't allow dogs on the islands, period (exclamation point!) So, if you and your dog are inseparable, don't bother applying to that district.

Indoor Pets

Our dog is an indoor dog. I can certainly see an advantage to having an indoor pet, versus an outdoor pet. Some larger dogs are left to roam free in our village, and I wouldn't send our dog outside alone for two minutes. A couple of our teachers have large dogs that stay tied-up outside their teacher housing units. They exercise the dogs regularly with long walks.

Every time we take our dog outside, he is on a leash. I want to be able to "reel him in" quickly if I need to. For this reason, he wears a harness, not a collar. We all three (myself, Mrs. Rose, and the dog) go out almost every day, and let the dog run around on the tundra. We have a 20-foot retractable leash that lets him scamper around and get the exercise he needs. He loves to hop and jump around in the snow and ice, so we make sure to check his fur for ice when we return.

Consider the weather if you plan to keep your dog outside in Alaska. The temperature can drop to -20 degrees F or colder, and the wind can drop the wind-chill to -50 degrees F or more.

Feeding Your Dog

You will need to have a supply of dog food or cat food for your pet. Your village store may sell this food, but the prices will be high, and the selection very limited. Once again, Amazon.com is a good place to start shopping for pet food. Several third-party vendors sell on Amazon, so make sure to consider shipping as part of the price.

Doggie Sweater and Jacket

Our 10-pound dog is not a hardy Alaska breed. So, he wears a dog sweater about all of the time – partly to keep him warm, and partly because he's cool like that. He also has an insulated parka that he wears when we go on our daily outings in the winter. Once again, major style props to the dog.

I have never actually seen a cat wear a sweater. Have you?

Life Without a Veterinarian

We don't have a doctor or a dentist in our village, so it follows that we don't have a veterinarian either. In fact, many of the regional hub cities don't have a full-time vet clinic. A veterinarian visits our regional hub one week every month and schedules appointments in advance by telephone. If you're bringing a pet to Alaska, here are some things to consider:

Work with your Current Vet

Before you move to the Alaska bush, schedule an appointment with your current veterinarian and talk with him/her about the move. Let them know that you won't have access to a veterinarian for the next few months. Ask them for advice that addresses your specific concerns. Perhaps they will be willing to accept your telephone calls on a fee-for-service (or maybe even free) basis.

Check for Vaccinations

Make sure to verify the expiration dates on your pet's vaccinations. You also want to make sure you have current copies of your pet's health records before moving to rural Alaska.

Plan for Veterinarian Visits in Anchorage or Fairbanks

If you're traveling through Anchorage or Fairbanks at Christmas or spring break, consider scheduling a veterinarian appointment. It's a good opportunity to have your pet examined, and his vaccinations updated. You can also obtain any required paperwork before leaving the state.

Traveling With Your Pet

My experience is with traveling with our 10-pound dog. Certainly there are Amazon books and web-sites dedicated to travel with pets, and you can easily find them online. Let me share a few things that experience has taught me.

How Will Your Pet Travel?

If you have a small dog or cat, your pet can probably travel as a carry-on item under the seat in front of you. This is how we travel with our dog, and it works just fine. In fact, most people are surprised to know that we even have a pet on the flight. Different airlines handle this differently. With some airlines, your pet carrier counts as your carry-on item or your personal item. Other airlines allow you the extra item.

A larger canine will not travel in the airplane cabin. You will need to contact the airline directly to arrange transportation for a large dog.

Contact the Airlines Early

You will probably buy your airline tickets online. Just as soon as that transaction is completed, call each airline that you will be using, and let them know that you will be traveling with a pet on the airplane. Most airlines limit the number of pets that they transport on each flight, and you need to make sure to reserve a slot for your pet.

Their first question will be about the size of the pet, and the conversation will diverge at that point. If your pet is small and will be traveling in the cabin, they will tell you about requirements for that scenario. If your pet is large, they will share that information as well. Either way, have a pen and paper in-hand when you make the call, because there will probably be some information that you will need to write down.

There will also be a fee collected to transport each pet. Some airlines collect the fee when you make your pet reservation, and other airlines collect the fee at the gate. You can expect to pay $75 to $125 to each airline that flies your pet.

Extra Cost –Per Airline!

Yes, you read that last sentence correctly. Each airline will collect the fee. So, let's say you are flying from Bethel, your regional hub, to your hometown of Lexington, Kentucky for Christmas break. You take airline "A" from Bethel to Anchorage, airline "B" from Anchorage to Chicago, and airline "C" from Chicago to Lexington. You might end up paying all three airlines' pet fee. And that's just one-way. You will be paying the fees on the return trip, too. Often these additional fees can nullify the savings from aggressive commando airline ticket shopping. When possible, investigate flying your complete route with one airline. The ticket may be a few dollars more, but the pet fee savings can make-up the difference. As always, the airline is the best resource for this information.

Dog or Cat Carriers

You will need to use a pet carrier to transport your pet. The airline will have the best information regarding the requirements for your carrier. They are the ones who will be flying your pet, so they are the authoritative source for information. Larger pet carriers can be purchased at major pet stores or online. When you go shopping, make sure you have the airline's requirements for transporting large animals with you. All retailers will advise you to check with your airline before purchase, and that's the advice I'm giving you.

If your pet will be flying in the cabin, then you have quite a few more options. Once again, your airline is the best resource for information about pet carriers. Your two choices for in-cabin pet carriers are hard-sided carriers that are basically smaller versions of the large travel kennels, and soft-sided carriers. Basically the carrier has to be small enough to fit below the seat in front of you. We have a soft-sided carrier that looks a lot like any other carry-on bag.

Some airlines have partnered with pet carrier companies to pre-approve certain small carriers. We bought a Sherpa brand carrier on Amazon.com for our pet. We fly Delta Airlines frequently, and our carrier has a Delta Airlines logo embossed on the side. Another reason I selected Sherpa was for their Guaranteed On-Board program. Your can enter your flight information and information about your pet at the Guaranteed On-Board web-site (www.flygob.com) and print a certificate that guarantees that the carrier is acceptable for the flight. Realize, of course, that they are just guaranteeing the carrier, and not the pet. Issues not related to the pet carriers (such as a sick pet or a late-arriving pet-owner) are not covered by the guarantee. The Guaranteed On-Board web-site does a good job of explaining the applications and limits of the guarantee.

Keeping Your Pet Happy In-flight

You've probably already thought about this, but I'll write it anyway. To keep your in-cabin pet comfortable on a long trip, you want put his favorite blanket and toys in the carrier for the trip. We carry a couple of extra dog chews in our carry-on, and give one to our dog if he gets a little restless. And while your want to keep your dog hydrated during the trip, you want to avoid giving an excess amount of water.

Our veterinarian prescribed a tranquilizing pill for our dog. We have used it, but to be honest he's fine without it. He's basically a relaxed little fellow. Must be the cool sweater!

Pottying at the Airport

If you have a long flight, or a series of long flights, you will probably want to give your in-cabin dog the opportunity to potty while at the airport. This is a great time to find one of those "Information" kiosks and ask. You won't be the first person to ask. I've noticed a recent trend in airports to accommodate this need. Some airports have designated park-like areas. Other airports will simply look the other way while your dog relieves himself in a secluded place in the ground transportation area. Okay, so it might not be pretty. But it is preferable to traveling with a canine who gives his "go out now" bark-and-yip signal throughout a five-hour flight.

The downside of giving your dog this opportunity at the airport is that it may mean exiting the secure area of the airport, and going through TSA security when you re-enter. Of course, you don't want to risk missing your connecting flight. Before leaving the secured airport area, you can probably find a TSA officer, tell him/her your plans, and ask how much time it typically takes to get through security. Do the math, and make the best choice for your pet, yourself, and your fellow passengers.

Flying to the Bush

Your flight to the bush will probably be on a local or regional airline. You will want them to know about your pet travel plans in advance as well. On the final flight to our village (on a Cessna 207 Skywagon) our dog rides in his carrier on Mrs. Rose's lap, at no extra charge. That's our experience – yours may be different. However, if you're fortunate enough to have two bush airlines flying to your village, the absence of an additional pet fee might help you decide which airline to patronize.

Teachers and administrators with large dogs and/or a large number of pets have been known to charter a flight to the village. This might sound extreme, but sometimes it represents the most reasonable and thrifty option. Once again, the number of passengers and the number of pets will determine the financials. Some bush airlines simply do not fly large animals as part of their regular passenger service.

Required Entry Paperwork

Most states have required veterinary paperwork when any animal – pet or otherwise – is brought into the state. Some states require a veterinarian exam within 10 days prior to travel. A state inspector has the authority to ask for the appropriate paperwork as you leave the airplane. We have traveled with a pet several times, and we have never been approached by an inspector. But every time we fly I have the required paperwork in my carry-on, just in case.

The news of this required paperwork actually came as a shock to me the first time we traveled south for Christmas. When I called the airline to reserve a space for our pet, the telephone agent notified me of this requirement. An Internet search revealed the specifics of our destination state – a veterinarian inspection within 10 days of arrival. I downloaded the forms. Fortunately, we had scheduled an extra day in Anchorage. We took a taxi to a 24-hour veterinary clinic, and an hour later we were on our way with the signed certificate. Because our trip was shorter than 10 days, the certificate was still good for our re-entry to Alaska.

As I wrote earlier, we have never been asked for the paperwork by a government official. But, I am glad I have always had it with me when flying to another state.

Keep a File Folder

Even if you don't consider yourself a tremendously organized person, I encourage you to keep a file folder or notebook containing all of your pet's paperwork. This file folder should include vaccination records, veterinarian receipts, previous inspection certificates, and confirmation numbers for your paid airline pet fees. I carry this folder with me when we travel with our dog.

Pets are an important part of many rural Alaska teachers' lives. Dogs and cats are always happy to see us when we get home. They don't ask too many questions, and they don't question the choices we make. They encourage us, get us out of bed in the morning, and make sure we get out of the house  every now and then. With proper planning, your pet can continue to provide companionship in the Alaska bush.

Just make sure to buy your dog a sweater.

Chapter 11

Questions to Ask During an Interview

I have interviewed for a few teaching positions in my life. Maybe you have, too. Typically a principal asks the questions, and the prospective teacher provides the answers. At the end of the interview, the principal typically asks, "Do you have any questions for me?" In most cases, the teacher asks a few questions (a) because it's expected, and (b) because it gives the teacher a chance to show that he's done some research about the school.

Some prospective teachers will ask a question designed to bring out a trait or skill that they could bring to the school. For example, a prospective teacher might ask, "What kind of recognition do you give to students who reach their reading goals?" The principal might respond, "Well, we don't really have a school-wide recognition program." This creates an opening for the prospective teacher to describe a successful reading recognition program that she administered at her previous school or during an internship. (That interview tip is a freebie from Uncle Wally!)

Great Big Changes

If you get a teaching job in your current city or town in the lower 48, you will probably keep the same house or apartment, and drive the same car. You will wear the same type of clothing, and shop at the same supermarket. Yes, after getting your first few paychecks, you might move into a nicer apartment, trade-in your college clunker for a new sub-compact, and switch to the national brand of orange juice. But by and large, your living situation will be about the same.

You probably see where I'm going here. Your move to rural Alaska will represent a near-total change in many areas of your life. (If you've read this book up to this point, you understand most of these changes.) Your new principal will also be your landlord. You may get a roommate you've never met. You'll no longer drive a car, and will use an ATV or shoe leather instead. Most of your food will come in the mail, and you will find yourself wearing a heavy parka and goose-down gloves every time you leave the house.

If you move to rural Alaska, your life will change. A great deal of that change will be the result of the village that you choose, and the living and working conditions there. So, you need to ask questions.

Asking Questions

Don't worry about offending the principal or the district recruiter. They expect you to ask questions. Most district recruiters will try to get to know their job candidates so that they can match the personality of the teacher to the characteristics of the community. Asking questions helps the principal and the recruiter understand who you are, and what's important to you. They want you to be happy. Happy teachers typically are better teachers. They return with another year of experience. And that's one less new teacher that the recruiter has to find.

Over the next few pages are some questions that you might consider asking the district recruiter and/or the principal. This list is by no means exhaustive. Please don't use it as a check-list, as some questions may not directly apply to your situation. Instead, use the list as starting point for your own list of questions. Remember to ask about things that are important to you.

The object here is to have no unhappy surprises when you reach your village. For example, you might have been hired to teach English, but later you find out that you will also be teaching PE and pre-algebra. Or when you arrive in teacher housing you find a composting toilet in the bathroom. Or you arrive in the village to find that your teacher housing is a mile away from the school. These situations certainly aren't deal-breakers, and I'm not suggesting that they downgrade your teaching experience. But you should know these things before accepting a job, not when your boots hit the ground.

Uncle Wally's Tip: Breaking a teaching contract and leaving the village before the contract ends ("quitting") should not enter into your plans. There is no "trial period" for teaching jobs. When you sign a contract, you are signing-on for the school year. Yes, there are true emergencies that make continuing employment impossible. If that's the case, you should immediately talk to your principal and your superintendent to work out a resolution. However, please don't think that if you don't like your village, you can just leave after a few weeks. You need to do the research before you go. Walking-off the job shouldn't be Plan B. The question, "Have you ever failed to complete a teaching contract?" appears on almost every teaching job application I've seen. You don't want to have to explain an error in judgment for your entire career. Get the facts before signing on the dotted line!

Questions to Ask During an Interview

"What is the job?"

Get a detailed description of the job you're interviewing for. The more specific details you can obtain, the more prepared you will be. Make sure that you know if the job is full-time or part-time.

"Am I contracting for placement in the school, or anywhere in the district?"

Some districts offer school-specific contracts. Others offer district-only contracts, allowing the district to place you in the school where they need you. This distinction is important if you've done extensive research on specific villages in the district.

"What is the Teacher Evaluation System in place?"

Teacher evaluation has recently become a critical issue in education. Teachers are retained and released based on their teacher evaluations. What criteria will be used to evaluate you? Some districts use widely-available tools, and other districts have created their own. Beware of evaluation instruments that place an extremely high percentage on achievement on standardized tests. Your teaching is more that how your students perform on one test one day.

"Can you describe the health care facility that I would use?"

As you read in Chapter 4, most villages have a village health clinic. If your village does not have a clinic for some reason, how are health care needs addressed? Are teachers welcome to use the village health clinic? It's kind of a running joke among Alaska teachers – we have the best health insurance in the nation, but we're 100 miles away from the nearest doctor.

"Does health insurance cover the summer? Will facilities in the lower-48 honor the health insurance?"

How does the health insurance work when you're not in the village, the district, or the state? Will you have coverage during summer break? What if you require emergency treatment in the lower 48? Will hospitals accept your insurance card? Don't create the impression that you're sickly, or that you run to the doctor every time you stub your toe. But these are reasonable questions to ask. Your fringe benefit package is part of your pay.

"What are the goals of the school?"

This is a good question for your principal. It shows that you are a team player and it lets the principal talk about something very familiar. Also, talking about the school's goals naturally creates an opening for you to talk about how you could help meet those goals.

"What is the school discipline plan?"

Approach this as a way to determine how the principal wants his teachers to handle discipline issues. If the principal responds that "all discipline issues are handled in the classroom," then that's a problem. Sometimes issues arise that require the principal to discipline students. If the school doesn't have a discipline plan, then look elsewhere.

"What is my teaching assignment?"

This will give you a feel for what the principal expects you to teach. Don't cringe if you're asked to pick-up a class that you don't have any experience with. I have taught PE, science, and pre-algebra in the bush. When I started, I didn't feel especially competent in any of those subject areas. But by the semester break I had learned to enjoy them.

"How likely is this assignment to change?"

Teaching assignments can change over the summer, and your principal would/should tell you that. You might be interviewing for a 5th grade position, but due to student enrollment you will teach a combined 4th-5th grade class. I would be skeptical of a principal who tells me that he/she is 100% sure that my teaching assignment won't change at least a little bit between the contract signing and the first day of school.

"What extra duties are assigned/expected?"

This is a good question for all teaching candidates, not just those applying to Alaska bush districts. Will you be expected to coach a basketball team? Sponsor the student council? Escort students to activities at the district level (overnight trips?) These opportunities may be appealing to you, or they may not. Either way, you should find out before accepting a position.

"What technology is available in the classroom? To the students?"

This question may or may not be important to you. I have always enjoyed using technology in my classroom. I can use a SmartBoard, and I can use a chalkboard. But I want to know what to expect in my classroom before the first day of school.

"What computer system is used?"

This is one of those "I want to be prepared" questions. Some districts are Mac-based, and some use Windows. If the school uses an operating system that you're not familiar with, you will want to spend at least part of the summer at a friend's house or at the public library learning to use a computer similar to the one you'll use at school. Many districts check-out a laptop computer to each teacher to use for the year. You want to be able to simply open the lid, press the power button, and start using your computer because there is no time for you to navigate a learning curve.

"Who would be a teacher willing to answer questions about living there?"

It's really nice to talk to a teacher who already works at the school. I had the opportunity to Skype with a teacher before accepting my most recent teaching position. Questions about the village store and the post office may be more appropriate for a colleague.

"Can you please describe teacher housing?"

This is your opportunity to get the complete picture of your teacher housing unit. Make sure to determine the size of the housing, number of bedrooms, and the extent of the plumbing. Is there hot water? How is the housing heated? What is the age of the housing? How far is the housing from the school? Will I have a roommate?

"Is my pet allowed in teacher housing?"

Certainly if you are a pet owner, you will want to ask this question early in the conversation.

"What is the cost of housing?"

Determine the cost of the housing, and what is included (utilities, etc.)

"What furnishings are in the housing unit?"

This will be your chance to learn about the furniture in your housing unit. Also, make sure to ask about things like drapes, a microwave oven, etc.

"How will I do my laundry?"

Does my housing unit have its own washer and dryer? Will I need to share? Do I need to do my laundry at school? Do I need to use the village laundry facilities?

"Can a friend or relative visit for a few days?"

This may or may not be a question that you will want to ask. However, you may have friends or family members who will want their own (brief) rural Alaska experience. Is it okay if they stay over for a few days?

"Is it possible/reasonable to leave the village over winter break? Spring break?"

This question is based more on weather than anything else. Does your village get snowed-in for several days at a time, thwarting holiday travel plans?

Remember, the list above is designed to stimulate your thinking about topics that are important to you. You will probably strike questions from the list, and add others of your own. Take plenty of notes during the interview, and make sure you have a thorough understanding of the job and the living situation before accepting a position.

Conclusion

Tough Questions Rarely Have Easy Answers

My goal in this book has been to provide you with information that will allow you to make a smooth transition to Alaska bush teaching, should you make that choice. I have tried to present the facts, so that you can make the best decision for yourself and your family.

I would not presume to make that decision for you, or influence your decision. No one else should, either. It's up to you. You can make the choice.

"Is moving to the Alaska bush really for me?" That's a tough question. And tough questions rarely have easy answers.

Former Alaska resident Tom Bodett may have said it best when he wrote, "In school, you're taught a lesson and then given a test. In life, you're given a test that teaches you a lesson."

If you choose to move to rural Alaska, it will be a test. It will teach you many lessons about yourself.

The conclusion of this book also represents the conclusion of my teaching career in rural Alaska. Mrs. Rose and I have decided to continue our lives in a less-remote location. I wanted to write this book while still living here in rural Alaska, so that the lessons I've learned about moving to Alaska and living in Alaska would be fresh in my mind, and I could share them with you.

We have had many great experiences in the Alaska bush, but now it's time to go.

Whatever you decide for your future, I wish you the best in your teaching career. Maybe you'll be in my classroom next year!

On behalf of the lovely Mrs. Rose, I remain sincerely...

Wally Rose

Illustration Credits

Made in the USA
Coppell, TX
20 October 2022

85033337R00125